Twenty-Five Scenic Road Walks in West Cork

G000255304

Twenty-Five
Scenic Road Walks
in West Cork

Seán Teegan

MERCIER PRESS

Mercier Press,
5 French Church Street, Cork
24 Lower Abbey Street, Dublin 1

© Seán Teegan

ISBN 1 85635 034 7

Acknowledgement

The author and publisher would like to thank Dundalgan Press for permission to quote excerpts from J C Coleman's *Journeys into Muskerry* and the Ordnance Survey of Ireland for the maps based on the Ordnance Survey, by permission of the government [permit no. 5713].

Contents

Introduction

In 1950 a paperback of 104 pages entitled *Journeys into Muskerry*[1] appeared on the shelves of bookshops here and there in Ireland. It did not rank amongst the bestsellers of the day and there is no record of the number of copies printed. A few years later it was out of print and has never been reprinted. Its author was a Corkman, J C Coleman, walker, mountaineer, naturalist, artist, amateur archaeologist. The paperback is a description, written with skill and affection, of that part of County Cork which is west of the city and extends towards the heads of the great bays of Roaringwater, Bantry and Kenmare in Kerry and north to the mountains which form the divide between the valleys of the Lee and Blackwater rivers – an area of some 500 square miles, comprising largely the old baronies of East and West Muskerry. It is the area known – in general terms – as West Cork. It is, to quote Coleman: 'an area, the most fascinating feature of which is the manner in which pastoral landscape, craggy bog-strewn country and actual mountains are so surprisingly intermingled ... the farther westward you go the wilder the scenery gets.'

Coleman journeyed through Muskerry on bicycle and on foot, frequently using public transport to get him and his bicycle from his home in Cork city to suitable starting points and his book is a delightful blend of geology, archaeology, history and scenery of the area together with superb pen-and-ink sketches by himself.

In the forty years which have passed since Coleman wrote about Muskerry, public transport has grown thinner and less frequent. Many miles of railway have been closed and the country bus that would carry your bicycle on its roof has long since gone. Many of the roads along which it was a delight to cycle or walk in Coleman's day are now cluttered

[1] J C Coleman, *Journeys into Muskerry*, Dundalgan Press

with cars and articulated trucks, each generating its own quantum of pollution. However, there are still miles and miles of byroads in Muskerry and beyond which are virtually devoid of vehicular traffic – apart from the occasional farm tractor – where it is possible to walk for maybe ten miles and meet as little as four or five vehicles. Unlike many European countries, Ireland does not have a network of public footpaths in country areas but in the case of West Cork this lack is easily compensated for by the density of the byroad network. The walks described in this book are on these byroads which wander up hill and down valley, through mountain gaps and across plains and on which every turn brings a new change of view in a region of unique scenery. The majority of the walks are circle walks and vary in distance from six to sixteen miles (10–25 km). The car is used to get from base to starting point.

The best centre from which to explore West Cork and the adjoining areas of Kerry through these walks is the town of Macroom but this should not put off the Cork city person from exploring the western half of the native county since each walk can be comfortably done in, at most, a twelve hour day and that includes the time taken to drive from Macroom and even from Cork city to the starting point and back. For each walk, therefore, clear directions are given for driving to the starting point from both Macroom and Cork.

In order to follow the walks and to derive maximum pleasure from them it is essential to become familiar with the relevant maps which are commercially available and this demands a basic knowledge of map reading (see p. 16). One is, thereby, enabled to keep at all times a broad overview of the various walking areas, to follow the walks described and to plan one's own variations on them. One is also enabled, with a little practice, to predict with considerable accuracy whether a given stretch of road is likely to be level or steep, what type of terrain is likely to be traversed and what the scenery is likely to be. The maps included in the text are for quick reference. They are all sections of the relevant maps mentioned below but should not be regarded as substitutes for them.

Each walk described has been walked by me at least three times – most of them many more times than that. This is because I enjoy them so much especially when I am introducing someone to a particular walk for the first time. I trust that, as a result of this familiarity, there are not too many errors.

Much of what follows in the next section may be 'old hat' and boring to the person already broadly familiar with the walking area and with the relevant maps. It has been included as an aid to the newcomer to walking and to Muskerry and also to visitors from abroad who, being walkers in their own country, are willing to extend their horizons on foot.

If you are fortunate to come by a copy of Coleman's work you will quickly see that mine is not a re-hash or an updating of it. Coleman does not describe precise walks, rather does he roam across the entire West Cork area and describe it with a far finer skill than does this book which is written specifically for the walker.

The first walk is close to Macroom and Cork and it is relatively short. Its starting point and route are easy to identify on the map and it has on its route a vantage point from which the entire walking area can be seen in perspective. The second walk is similar to the first but requires a little more skill in map-reading. The remaining 23 walks are grouped according to the mountain range in which they are located: the Boggeraghs, the Derrynasaggarts and the Shehys.

This is a book for the 'ordinary' walker, the not-so-young as well as the young who want to enjoy unique scenery without the strain associated with the more spectacular and strenuous routes across bogland and mountain-top where one frequently has to concentrate on foothold or direction finding. It is also a book for all seasons of the year. The much maligned Irish climate has the great advantage of offering superb walking days right through the year, even in mid-winter. The only extra point to remember for winter walking is the earlier onset of darkness.

My sincere thanks go to my wife, Maura, who has been

my walking companion for half a century; to my colleague Professor John A Murphy who – as we walked the twenty-five walks together – kept prodding me to write this book; to Michael Murphy, cartographer, Geography Department, University College, Cork, whose patience I frequently tried; and to Deirdre Sheehan whose word-processing skills transformed my illegible handwriting.

SEÁN TEEGAN

The Walking Area

An idea of the extent of the total walking area may be obtained by having a look at one of the maps to be discussed in the section on Maps namely the one entitled Ireland South, Number 4 of the 1: 250,000 Holiday Map Series. With the help of ruler and pencil you obtain an irregular seven-sided figure by joining the following points and this gives you the periphery of the walking area: The seven corners of the figure are i) Mourne Abbey (157 093),[1] which is about three-quarters of the way along the straight line joining Cork city and Mallow, ii) Banteer (139 099), iii) Rathmore (117 094), iv) Kenmare (091 071), v) Glengarriff (093 056), vi) Bantry (100 048), vii) Dunmanway (124 053). The enclosed area is about 500 square miles (140,000 hectares). As can be seen from the map the area contains a considerable amount of high ground (coloured dark brown) embodying, as it does, the three mountain ranges of Muskerry – the Boggeraghs in the east, the Derrynasaggarts followed by the Shehys in the west. Some of the walks in these ranges go as high as 1,000 feet (330 m) with the result that many of the long-distance views stretch far beyond the walking area resulting in a very extensive viewing area, the rough boundaries of which may be drawn by connecting the following points: i) Dungarvan (226 094), ii) Tipperary (189 136), iii) Camp, on the north shore of the Dingle peninsula (070 110), iv) Cahersiveen (046 079), v) Mizen Head (073 023). The first walk takes one to a high point, Knockane by name, which is just over 8 miles from Macroom and from which a very fine general view of almost the entire walking area and much of the viewing area may be obtained.

It is, perhaps, an exaggeration to refer to the Boggeraghs, Derrynasaggarts and Shehys which form the backdrop to the

---

[1] *Numbers in parenthesis are grid references (see p 17).*

view from Knockane as mountain ranges since there is no point in them over 2,300 feet (700 m). Thus one is never dwarfed by them even when one is close to them. Neither is one ever threatened by sharp angular peaks because glaciers, rain and wind have combined to give their sandstone summits a rounded and inviting aspect. Time was when these peaks were almost completely wooded but centuries of felling have exposed their stony heights. Re-afforestation is, however, slowly reversing matters and large areas of their slopes are now covered in trees albeit of an alien species.

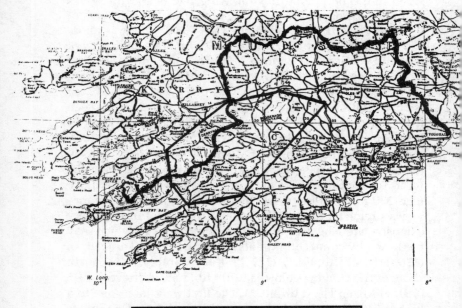

THE WALKING AREA

Periphery of Walking Area: ▬▬▬▬
Cork–Kerry Boundary: ▬▬▬▬▬

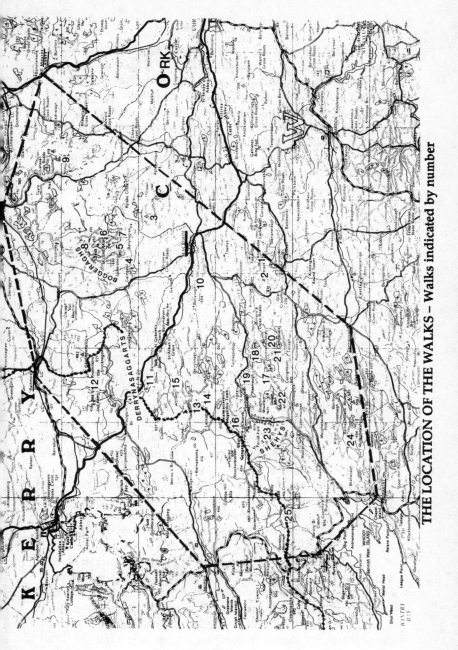

THE LOCATION OF THE WALKS – Walks indicated by number

Throughout the year clouds from the Atlantic Ocean drift across the landscape, often sitting on the peaks, often blending with the highlands and lowlands and the blue of the sky to give ever-changing panoramas of colour and shadow. They discharge their moisture over the mountains and onto the plains thus imparting a soft light to the countryside. Much, but not all, of this moisture directly feeds the many streams that cascade down from the heights, each cutting its own valley. On the southern slopes of the Boggeraghs and the Derrynasaggarts these streams make their way to the Lee river whilst on the northern slopes they join the Blackwater. The streams of the Shehys follow a slightly more complex pattern in contributing to the Lee, the Bandon and directly to Bantry Bay. That moisture which does not contribute directly to the streams is trapped in the bogs and heavy soils to be released much later to the streams so that even in periods of low rainfall the walker always has the company of the flowing stream.

The beautiful green pastures in the lower regions are really the result of man's activity. Man has lived off the land here for over 6,000 years and everywhere one finds evidence of his works. The golden furze (gorse) of the spring and the purple heather of the autumn on the hillsides are the result of over-grazing which may well have been necessary to sustain a large population. The hawthorn, the blackthorn and the elder and the multitude of colourful hedgerow plants are the direct result of man's efforts to enclose fields just as are the stone walls on the higher levels.

There is abundant evidence that, in the distant past and even in the recent past, the area sustained a far higher population than it does today. For this evidence one need not look further than the dense network of roads, many of which figure in the walks to follow. These roads are not the work of local authorities or governments. They have been made by walking feet and many of them have been there for centuries and millions of people have trod them. And they are not confined to the low-lying areas. Many of them wind their way up into the mountains searching for the col, the pass or the gap near the top to make the going to the other side that bit easier.

To experience and enjoy the sights, the slopes, the colours, the sounds and the solitude of this unique area one has to walk it. There is no other way. Even the push-bike is at times too fast and an encumbrance. Most of the byroads out here were made by and for feet and not for wheels.

Maps and Related Topics

You, the walker, will require three maps – all of them published by the Ordnance Survey of Ireland and easily available in tourist offices, book shops, and newsagents. Reference has already been made to one of them in the previous section, namely sheet Number 4, Ireland South. This is one of four maps which cover the entire island of Ireland. The series has recently been published for the first time and the scale is a metric one, namely 1 centimetre (cm) of map is equivalent to 2.5 kilometres (km) of distance. The Representative Fraction (R. F.) is 1: 250,000 which means 1 unit of length on the map equals 250,000 of the same units of actual distance (i.e. 1 cm = 2.5 km). These are not walking maps since their scale is too small to give the necessary detail. But sheet Number 4 (referred to henceforth as 'Ireland South sheet') is essential since it covers the entire walking area and, in addition, the entire area that can be viewed from the walks. Since it is really a motorist's map it will also enable you to plot your route from base (Macroom/Cork) to the starting point of each walk. Furthermore it is a 'Relief' map, that is, by the use of suitable colouring high ground is easily distinguished from low ground and the heights in metres (m) of most of the mountain peaks are clearly marked. All main roads are clearly indicated by number.

When it comes to suitable walking maps one has to rely on Sheets 21 (Kerry–Cork) and 24 (West Cork) of what is known as the half inch (0.5 in) series – a series of 25 maps covering the entire island and having a R. F. of 1: 126,720 or 0.5 in of map is equivalent to 1 mile of actual distance. It is unfortunate that this lack of uniformity of scale exists at present between the Ireland South sheet and the walking sheets but no resolution exists. It should be noted however that the Ordnance Survey Office has begun to publish a complete set of very fine large-scale metric maps for the entire island. The R.F. of this series is 1: 50,000 i.e. 1 cm of map equals 0.5 km of actual distance – ideal for the detail required by the walker. However, at the time of writing, the sheets relevant here have not appeared.

Like the Ireland South map, Sheets 21 and 24 are relief maps but the larger scale allows for considerable detail of height (in feet, of course) especially as far as the contour lines (lines joining points of equal height) are concerned and, by following the layout of these contour lines, one is – with a little experience – able to pick out mountain passes and gaps, to determine the slope of hills and other high areas and to determine how steeply or gently a road rises or falls. The heights of mountain peaks are marked as well.

These 0.5 in maps are based on the survey of Ireland undertaken over 150 years ago. Although they have been revised and reprinted many times they are not fully up-to-date in every detail. The latest revision/reprinting was made in the late 1980s and all the roads – with 2 minor exceptions – cited in all the walks are marked on these latest reprintings and this makes them invaluable – indeed necessary – for the walker. The following paragraphs contain important information and advice in regard to the interaction of map and walk and they refer particularly to the 0.5 in maps. The reprint date is given as the Government Copyright date at the foot of each sheet.

Legend: The map legend gives details of scale, of symbols, abbreviations, etc used. It is useful for you to become familiar with these. This familiarity will, in turn, enrich the pleasures of the walk. The legend also indicates the direction on the map of North (towards the top of the sheet) and this should be remembered as frequent references are made to the compass points.

National Grid: The National Grid provides an easy and convenient means of identifying, with considerable accuracy, any point on a map. Grid References (G. R.) will be used to identify important points on the route of the walks such as starting points and crossroads where there is a change of direction which could otherwise be difficult to find. Each of the maps referred to carries a full explanation of the National Grid and of the means for determining Grid References and these should be carefully read and understood. In all the Grid References quoted the last figure in each of the two co-ordinates (the Easting and the Northing) is an estimate but a necessary one.

One further point here: on first glance, it may appear that Grid References on the Ireland South sheet are different from those on the 0.5 in sheets. They are in fact the same – the apparent difference arising from the difference in scale.

Miles versus Kilometres: Since the walking maps are based on an inch/mile scale then all distances quoted in the accounts of the walks are in miles and all heights in feet (ft). This may appear to be going against the general trend especially since, at the time of writing, all signposts are being altered from miles to kilometres. However it is felt that the over-ruling factor is the map. Furthermore, people of whom you ask for a direction or distance will quote you in miles. In rural Ireland the mile will die hard.

Approximate conversion factors are as follows:

To Convert	Multiply By
miles to kilometres	1.6
kilometres to miles	0.6
feet to metres	0.3
metres to feet	3.0
inches to centimetres	2.5
centimetres to inches	0.4

Main Roads: Main roads very seldom form part of the walks although many references are made to them especially in regard to getting from base to starting point. These roads are clearly marked in all the maps. They are classified as N (National) or R (Regional) followed by a number. For example, the main road from Cork to Macroom is the N22 and the main road from Macroom to Millstreet is the R582. Some of the older printings of sheets 21 and 24 carry the pre-EC road classification system based on Trunk (T) and Link (L).

Place Names: Most place names in the walking area are old Irish names which have taken on an English form. As far as the maps are concerned the names of many places are given rather grim phonetic spellings. The original survey was, after all, undertaken by Englishmen who frequently picked up the name by ear from the native Irish speaker and gave it a phonetic English spelling. Furthermore, different spellings of the same place name often appear on different signposts and these in turn often differ from that on the map. However, the advent of the km signpost has cleared the air somewhat in this latter regard. A good example of the discrepancies which have applied heretofore is the spelling of the starting point of Walk 1. Teerelton on Sheet 24, Tarelton on one signpost, Tereltin on another – all corruptions of the Irish Tir Eltin (Eltin's land). In the text which follows all place names are spelt exactly as on the maps no matter how garbled they may be. This is in the interests of clarity.

It is hoped that the above rather lengthy section on maps and relevant matters will not discourage the would-be walker. These points have been raised to make the going easy and pleasant and to avoid errors. There is nothing worse than being unable to find the starting point of a walk or finding oneself on the wrong road and, as a result having to retrace one's steps adding, thereby an unwelcome extra mileage to that of the walk.

Useful Hints

Homework: Having decided beforehand on a particular walk it will add much to its enjoyment if you read the account of it right through before starting and also follow it in the map. It is useful to put an easily identifiable pencil mark on the starting point so that when you refer to the map en route you can readily find where you are relative to the marked starting point.

Weather: In spite of the size and position of Ireland in the northern hemisphere, weather forecasts are pretty accurate. Do not set out – especially on the longer walks – unless good weather is forecast. Therefore, keep an eye/ear on the television/radio forecast. The weather forecast for the forthcoming 24 hours for south-west Ireland may be obtained by telephoning 1550 123 850.

What to Wear: No special clothing is necessary except, perhaps a light raincoat and cap/hat as protection against the sudden shower. By way of footwear, a pair of strong, comfortable, waterproof shoes or boots with thick soles is adequate. Occasionally it is inevitable that one will get what is known as 'a good wetting'. However, it is amazing how quickly one dries off when walking if there is a break in the downpour. A wetting should happen very seldom if you keep an eye/ear on the forecast. A change of clothing in the boot of the car can, at times, be a comfort to look forward to.

What to Carry: The maps of course. A pocket compass and light binoculars are well worth considering. These items and any rain gear and sustenance are best carried in a shoulder bag so that the arms are free apart from any restriction caused by a walking stick which is part and parcel of the good walker. The stick is useful as a defence against barking dogs. Most rural homesteads have at least one dog. The dogs may give you a noisy welcome as you approach their terrain but very seldom will they attack. Do not threaten them with your stick. Just let them see it and if necessary point it towards them. That will be enough for them to keep their distance. Pocket sized dog repellers are now commercially available. They emit a supersonic sound which really makes dogs scuttle off very quickly.

Parking the Car: For each walk helpful information is given in regard to parking close to the starting point. You will often find yourself parking on narrow roads so leave good room for passing traffic. No matter how remote the area do not park on corners or at crossroads unless there is plenty of space. Local people frequently when driving do not expect to find parked cars and tend to take sharp corners. Furthermore, do not park across gateways no matter how disused they may appear to be.

Walking Pace: At the conclusion of the account of each walk the distance and the approximate walking time are given. The latter is very approximate. In fact it is little more than an indicator. Adopt the pace that suits you best but do not stroll as this will tire you quickly. Give yourself plenty of time to enjoy the scenery. Above all, do not be constricted by a time limit.

Local Traffic: Although most of the roads traversed in the walks are very minor roads and carry very little vehicular traffic, nevertheless be that bit careful when you hear approaching traffic. Many of the roads are narrow and the very last thing a driver may expect to meet is a walker.

The People you will Meet: One thing here is certain. You will meet very few, if any, pleasure walkers like yourself. You will meet locals (but not many) on foot or on bicycle moving cattle or rounding up sheep. A barking dog will sometimes bring the woman of the house to the door to see who is approaching. The ordinary people of West Cork and Kerry are warm, friendly and welcoming. They meet very few walkers and may often be surprised to learn that you have walked or are about to walk so far.

Should you require direction do not produce your map and say 'Where am I?' Most of these good people have no use whatever for maps nor do they know the roads by number. They know where the roads go to and the direction in which they go and, of course, they will quote you distances in miles.

Much of what is written above will not be new to the few who are already country walkers and familiar with rural Ireland and maps. It is hoped that the inclusion of it will help both novices from home and visitors from abroad to enjoy the pleasure of country walking amidst beautiful surroundings.

Go dté tú slán is go n-éirigh an bóthar leat.

1

A Triangle Walk South of Teerelton

This relatively short walk of about 6 miles has been selected as the first one for a number of reasons namely i) it starts and finishes in the hamlet of Teerelton which is easily identified in the top right-hand corner of Sheet 24 (its G.R. is W 318 656) and it is only 8 miles from Macroom and 23 miles from Cork city, ii) being easy to follow, it offers a good introduction to map reading, iii) it is almost entirely on narrow roads with green spines on which there is little traffic and iv) at its highest point, Knockane 858 ft, there is an unsurpassed view of the area which encompasses the walks in this book and of much else as well.

Before commencing a description of the walk it would be a good idea to trace it on the map (Sheet 24). Teerelton (which has as many spellings as there are signposts directing to it – and there are many) consists of a cross of 5 roads around which are a pub-cum-shop, a co-op store, a substantial parochial house (the nearest church is about 2 miles to the west in the townland of Cooldorrogha) and a school a short distance along the road to Cappeen. The walk follows the road to the south-east out of Teerelton up to Knockane (marked on the map), a distance of about 1 mile. Near the top it goes through a crossroad. It now falls to a junction (G.R. W 332 620) where one turns right on the road running north-east back up to the cross near Knockane from which it goes back down the hill to Teerelton.

From Cork the easiest way (and there are many) to Teerelton is to take the N22 Macroom road to a crossroad (G.R. W 390 680 – this stretch of the N22 is on Sheet 25) 1 mile beyond the hamlet of Lissardagh. The cross – known as Dooniskey Cross – is easily identified by the large buff-coloured house on the right-hand side of the main road. If

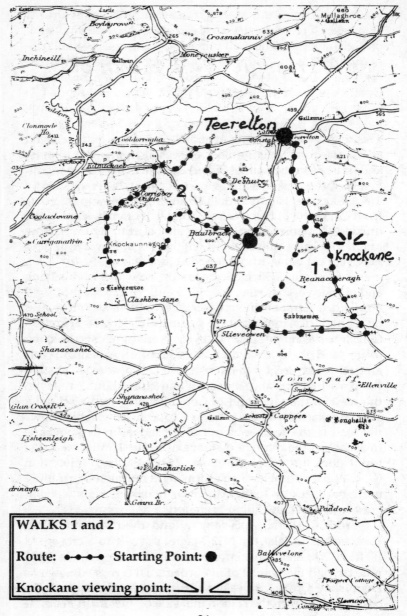

WALKS 1 and 2

Route: •••• Starting Point: ●

Knockane viewing point: ⌐⌐

you are starting from Macroom take the N22 eastward. At Dooniskey Cross take the narrow road to the south and sign-posted Teerelton. The road immediately bridges a small tributary of the Lee. Continue straight through the first cross-road and at the second crossroad (about 0.75 mile from Dooniskey) turn right signposted to Toames. For about 1.75 miles you are on a level, lightly-wooded road. You follow the signpost to Teerelton after which the road begins to rise gently and wind. Having avoided a junction to the left you soon come to a signpost (3.3 miles from Dooniskey) to Enniskeane, the direction of which you follow. You are now on a gently-rising and winding road which finally breaks into a long straight gradual rise to Teerelton. As you approach the hamlet (about 2 miles from the last signpost) notice the rounded hill ahead of you. This is Deshure which figures much in Walk 2. There is plenty of car-parking space near the co-op store.

In addition to Sheet 24 it would be worthwhile to bring along Sheet 21 and the Ireland South sheet together with your compass and – if available – a pair of binoculars.

With 5 roads all converging together it is important to select the correct one. Stand, therefore, with your back to the south wall of the pub and facing the co-op store. The road for you is the one facing you. As you start up this rising road the co-op store is on your left. Having passed a few homes on the left the road begins to wind and climb that bit more steeply with the view to the west (right) getting better all the while. Having ascended steadily for about 1 mile you come to the crossroad already mentioned. The road on the right is the one on which you will return but just now go straight through up to the top of the hill where the road swings left.

Now, look back at one of the great views in Co. Cork. Bearing in mind the importance of the view in relation to all the subsequent walks and rather than break the continuity of this walk, it is discussed in detail on page 27. Suffice it to say here that, as your eye wanders from north-east (right) to south-west (left) it sweeps out an unbroken view through an angle of 230 degrees. Although this is the highlight of the walk remember it is but the highlight. Ahead of you there are still many views of parts of the great one.

Continue along the now level road and enjoy the pleasant views of Shehy mountain and Nowen off on your right. About 0.5 mile from the summit the road falls sharply and ultimately crosses a stream after which it rises to a junction where you turn right onto the road with the green spine. This road runs due west.

Soon on your right you pass a homestead with a very attractive stone wall and gate piers. Forestry can now be seen ahead on the right and you pass a cottage on the left with a remarkable standing stone in front of it. Very soon straight ahead of you the hump of Shehy mountain appears in the distance. Carry on until you come to the crossroad where you turn right. At this point if you look at the map you will see another crossroad about 0.5 mile further on to the west at Slieveowen where a right turn would bring you directly into Teerelton. There is traffic and there are no views on this road.

You now have ahead of you 2 miles of a really delightful, rising road with a green spine. On the left notice some ornate wrought-iron gates. When you come to the one with the spoked wheel, look over it and enjoy the view all the way from the eastern end of the Derrynasaggarts around to Shehy on the left. Having passed some forestry on the left and about 1.5 miles from the crossroad you will see a very narrow road going off to the right and rising. This is a culde-sac (although the map indicates it as a through road) but just walk up the few yards to the crest to enjoy almost the same great view as you did at Knockane but now from a different angle and with a different light on it.

Retrace your steps to the junction and having turned right, continue on your course enjoying the scenery ahead. If the day is clear you should catch another glimpse of Macgillycuddy's Reeks shortly before the road begins to descend to the cross below Knockane where you turn left. The downhill mile to Teerelton is scenery all the way.

Distance: 6 miles. Walking time (exclusive of viewing time): about 2 hours.

You could, of course, have driven up to that cross below Knockane instead of leaving the car at Teerelton. However, parking is difficult in the vicinity of the cross and you would miss those magnificent views on that final mile down to Teerelton which can be enjoyed only when walking.

Walking the triangle in reverse by turning right at the cross below Knockane is equally rewarding if not more so as you have the great view ahead of you from Knockane to Teerelton.

The View from Knockane

The best view point is that obtained by scrambling up on the ditch on your right (as you face the view) where there is a little plateau on which two people can stand in comfort. It can be breezy up here and you may have difficulty in holding the map open. You would have a little more shelter standing on the grassy margin on the left hand side of the road.

For a preliminary 'survey' the map to have in front of you is the Ireland South Sheet as this covers the entire expanse of view. Later if you wish to do a more detailed survey you could change to Sheets 21 (the Boggeraghs and the Derrynasaggarts) and 24 (the Shehys and further south).

The compass will clearly identify north as running through the broad 'trough' between mountainy slopes on either side of it. This 'trough' (600 ft) carries the Macroom–Millstreet road (R582) and forms the divide between the Boggeragh mountains on the right (east) the Derrynasaggart mountains on the left (west).

The lower of the 2 outstanding peaks of the Boggeraghs is Musherabeg and the higher is Musheramore. The rounded top which lies down somewhat on the right-hand slope of Musheramore is Mushera and the slight dip just near to this marks the course of the Butter Road (Walk 6) as it reaches its highest point between Cork and Millstreet. The map will make it clear to you that there are more peaks in the Boggeraghs than those mentioned but they are not visible from your view point. Walks 3–9 will bring you into Boggeragh country.

Moving further to the right Knockabrocka stands out on the skyline behind a cluster of trees in the immediate foreground while the high land stretching on either side of it is the Barrahaurin area through which runs the Cork–Banteer road (R579). If, from the top of the ditch, you cast your eye away to the right (50 degrees east of north) you should see against the skyline the outline of the Galtee mountains in Co. Tipperary (40 miles from you).

Turning now to the left of the Macroom–Millstreet road we enter Derrynasaggart country (Walks 10–15) starting with the long gradual rise to the first major peak – Mullaghanish with its TV/Radio relay mast. The twin villages of Ballymakeera and Ballyvourney lie at the southern foot of Mullaghanish. Moving further to the left the eye is attracted to the twin peaks (the highest in the range) aptly known as the Paps. A dip immediately to the right of the right-hand Pap indicates the highest point on the old road from the Clydagh valley to 'The City' (Walk 12). The left-hand Pap slopes gradually down to the Macroom–Killarney road (N22) at a point a mile or so south of Glenflesk. As in the case of the Boggeraghs, there is more to the Derrynasaggarts than what meets the eye here. In particular there is Caherbarnagh, the next highest peak after the Paps which is completely obscured by Mullaghanish but which is a most impressive looking pile when viewed from the north (Blackwater valley).

After the Paps, the Derrynasaggart range curves south and hence that bit closer to you and the mountains which you see further away to the left of the Macroom–Killarney road really belong to what may be called the eastern end of the Kerry mountains, the jagged peak being Crohane near Lough Guitane followed by the large elongated hump of the Mangerton massif (about 50 degrees west of north). If the day is clear away beyond Mangerton you should be able to see a group of 4 or 5 closely-spaced peaks tilted towards the east. These are the Macgillycuddy's Reeks amongst which is Carrauntwohill – Ireland's highest mountain. As the crow flies the Reeks are about 25 miles from you.

Moving to the left of the Kerry mountains, and some-

28

what nearer, the Derrynasaggart range turns into a wall-like stretch of high ground soon cut by a dip in the vicinity of (what is left of) Coom Wood where the scenic road from Ballyvourney via Coolea to Inchee and Morley's Bridge passes at about 1,000 ft from Cork to Kerry (Walks 13 and 15). Next you should be able to identify (binoculars would help) the huge cliff face of Foilanumera with its vertical gashes.Then comes the rather flattened top of Mweelin followed soon (in the farther distance) by that peak which is shaped like an ocean wave about to topple (to the right). This is Coomataggart which towers above you on your left as you tread (Walk 13) the old road from Ballingeary to Morley's Bridge high up near Lackabaun.

As the eye now moves further to the south-west you come into the Shehy mountains the environs of which you will explore in Walks 16–25. What at once catches the eye to the left is that ugly 'aloof Matterhorn-looking peak' (Coleman, *Journeys into Muskerry*) known as Shehy Mountain (pronounced locally as 'Shehe'). Although it is less than 1,800 ft it can be seen clearly from the northern suburbs of Cork city. Strangely enough it is not named on any of the Ordnance Survey maps although its height (545 m, 1,797 ft) is marked. Shehy mountain is the greatest landmark in West Cork. It is the highest of a trio of peaks which are quite close together and are in a line running in a north-east to south-west direction south of the river Lee near Ballingeary. The second peak, Douce mountain (named on the maps), is the one to the right of Shehy. The third, Doughill, is not easily visible from your vantage point. It is a little further to the right from Douce and blends too well with the heights surrounding the Pass of Keimaneigh and Gougane Barra. A shoulder on the left-hand side of Shehy falls down to a pronounced dip. This is Cousane Gap which carries the road (R585) from Crookstown (12 miles west of Cork city) via Cappeen and Kealkill to Bantry Bay. This road used to be known along its length as the 'Bantry Line'.

Before passing on from the Shehy mountain area notice the high elongated hump of heath in front of the dip between Shehy and Douce: this is Carrigarierk – the pivot of

Walk 20. It is worth noting too that from where you are Douce is due west of you and if you could see away across the heights behind Douce, you would see Coomhola Mountain and Priestsleap (Walk 25) which is regarded here as the western end of the Shehy range.

The next distinctive peak some distance to the left (25 degrees south of west) is Nowen Hill. From where you are standing it looks like a somewhat smaller version of Shehy. It is a few miles north of Drimoleague and is the source of the Bandon river. As the eye follows on down the western slope of Nowen it lights on a peak in the farther distance. This is Mullaghmesha close to the hamlet of Castle Donovan and the high ridge further to the west carries the old road from Dunmanway to Bantry. Walk 24 takes you into this fascinating country. The final rounded height worth noting further to the left is Mount Kid which forms the eastern end of the mountains (including Mount Gabriel) which comprise the Mizen peninsula.

One is now looking along a line which is roughly 30 degrees south of west and as the eye moves still further south it can still see land but it is relatively low land comprising, as it does, what lies north of the Clonakilty–Skibbereen–Ballydehob road (N71). In fact one can see due south which puts one in line with Galley Head – one of the land-falls for ocean traffic coming east across the North Atlantic.

Your eye has now surveyed a fair cross-section of county Cork especially West Cork. In fact you have scanned from the Galtees (50 degrees east of north) to Mount Kid (35 degrees south of west) and beyond to due south – a total of 230 degrees out of the full circle of 360 degrees. But do not pass on just yet and say 'That's that'. Time should not dominate you here. Let your eye wander back from south towards the east and familiarise yourself with the landmarks of the three mountain ranges within which are most of the walks in this book. The sun's angle will have changed since you commenced your survey and other distant features will now be lit and you will see much that you missed on the first scan.

Before pressing on with the walk have a look at the foreground. It is one of ever green, fertile rolling country falling away towards the Lee valley in the north although the river itself is not visible. Finally have a look at what is immediately in front of you namely that rounded green hill known as Deshure followed on your left by a broad concavity which rises up to Knockaunnagorp. The next walk (2) takes you into the pleasant country surrounding these two hills and will afford you many fine views far and near.

If you wish to experience what may be the best view of all from Knockane drive up there on a hard frosty night in winter, early spring or late autumn (during the rest of the year there will be a trace of daylight in the sky even at midnight). Select a night on which there is no moon and just look at the heavens at a spot where there are no ground lights to dim their splendour. There are as many Irish versions of Teerelton as there are English spellings. One of them is Tir Realtan – Land of Constellations!

2

Deshure and Knockaunnagorp

As pointed out in Walk 1 this walk is also centred in the
Teerelton area. Like Number 1, it is relatively short but unlike it, it requires a little more careful map-reading (Sheet
24). In traversing the slopes of Deshure and the heights of
Knockaunnagorp (hillock of the bodies) it offers differing
looks at parts of that great view from Knockane and wanders through quiet and pleasant countryside.

To get to the starting point drive south from Teerelton
on the Cappeen road passing the school on the right. Ignore
the first turn to the right (not marked on the map) which is a
cul-de-sac leading to a farm high up on Deshure. The next
road to the right is about 0.75 mile from Teerelton and is indicated on the map by two closely spaced lines. This junction
is the starting point but, for convenience of parking drive on
the extra few yards to the next junction to the right near a
cottage. This is the finishing point and there is parking on
the grassy verge on the left-hand side of the Cappeen road.
The G.R. of the junction at which you now are is W 312 638.

Walk back the short distance to the previous junction
and turn left down the falling road with its green spine. It
continues to fall for just over 0.25 mile and offers inviting
views of the Shehy range to the west. A fairly steep climb up
the western slope of Deshure now follows to about 700 ft
where there is a farmstead and also the first of the fine views
to be encountered. This one is to the south and west. To the
south the land slopes towards Cappeen and beyond across
the valley of the Bandon river to the high land which inter-
venes between it and the coastline in the Rosscarbery–
Glandore region. In the west cone-shaped Douce stands out
and further in the distance to the right the sharp bluff of
Coomataggart and the high land near Keimaneigh and Gou-

gane Barra. In the foreground is the lightly-wooded hump of Knockaunnagorp. As you come around the crest of the hill and turn north almost the entire Derrynasaggart range faces you off in the distance.

Follow the now sharply-falling road until it meets the Teerelton–Kilmichael road onto which you turn left on the gentle decline with good views of both Shehy and Douce. Follow this road for about 0.5 mile (for safety keep an eye on your progress on the map) passing a junction on the right, then shortly afterwards a junction on the left, then over a bridge (spanning a little tributary on its way north to the Lee), immediately after which you will come to a junction to the left which you take. Just between the bridge and the junction there are, on your left, the remains of a dancing platform now almost completely hidden by greenery.

Your narrow road soon begins to climb up past Carrig-boy Castle (map) – now a homestead surrounded by mature trees. Shortly before the 'Castle' the road swings west and for about 0.25 mile it has a lovely line of beech trees along its right-hand side which form a series of arcades through which to admire the distant panorama of the Derryna-saggarts to the north. In the foreground you should be able to identify Cooldorragha church on a little height. Having passed the line of trees you now have a broader view of the Derrynasaggarts and even of distant Mangerton while away to the east the peaks of the Boggeraghs are in sight. Ignore the junction to the right and continue the climb.

As you approach the top of Knockaunnagorp the vista suddenly changes as the landscape to the west opens on your right and the Shehy mountains replace the Derryna-saggarts – (from right to left) Doughill, Douce (cone), Shehy and Nowen. This grand view stays with you to the top and down part of the steep decline. In less than 0.5 mile from the top the road has begun to level out and you come to a cross where you turn left onto a narrower road. This is a quiet and pleasant road but since it is low-lying it offers no great distant views along its length of about 1.5 mile when at a T junction you turn right onto a wider and obviously more used road. This road gradually rises and within a mile joins

33

the Teerelton–Cappeen road at the point where you left the car.

Distance: 6 miles. Time: about 2 hours.

Although we now move away from the Teerelton area it should be realised that there is still plenty of good walking here especially to the south and west and by studying the dense road network on the map it is possible to plan quite a few good circular walks.

The Boggeragh Mountains

Boggeragh Mountains in large capitals on the lower half of Sheet 21 easily identifies the area of the next 7 walks. On the west, the area is bounded by the Macroom–Millstreet road (R582), on the north by the Blackwater river, on the east by the Mallow–Coachford road (R619) and on the south by the river Lee.

Although the highest point (Musheramore) is a mere 2118 ft nevertheless there are no fewer than fourteen points in the area above 1000 ft. Boggeragh country is somewhat bleak since it contains much moorland but this moorland is seldom unattractive as it is broken by the green fields of the many little river valleys which reach up into it from the lower areas. Of late large tracts of it have been re-afforested thus restoring it to what it originally was prior to the whole-sale felling of recent centuries.

The strength of the Boggeraghs as walking-country is twofold. Firstly since most of the walks are above 800 ft there are many and varying long-distance panoramas in all directions and secondly the entire area is criss-crossed by a vast network of byroads, many of them with green spines – criterion of little vehicular traffic.

The whole area is now very thinly populated but in past times the opposite was the case. The large number of stone-alignments in the area is evidence of a large pre-Christian population whilst the road density and the vast number of derelict homesteads point to a high population in later centuries and hand-built stone walls still enclose moorland which was one time pasture.

Note: The routes of all the Boggeragh walks are completely within the limits of Sheet 21 and all map references in the text are to this sheet. Furthermore, since all the grid references are in the W Sub-Zone the letter W will be omitted from quoted grid references.

THE BOGGERAGH WALKS

Route: •━•━•━•   Starting Point: ●

Getting to Boggeragh Country: ▬▬▬

Getting to Boggeragh Country: More precisely getting to the starting points of the various walks. Since Macroom is at the south-western corner of the area, the route from there will be described.Travellers from Cork can take the main road (N 22) to Macroom, drive through the main street passing the Castle on the left and over the 9-arch stone bridge which crosses the Sullane river and immediately turning right onto the road signposted to Ballinagree. Immediately after passing the older homes of Masseytown, the road begins to rise, very soon passing newer homes on the left. Just short of 2 miles from the bridge ignore the road to the left signposted 'Coilte Teo' and continue straight through the next crossroads still following the signpost to Ballinagree on the gradually rising road which soon comes out into open country and arrives at Bawnmore Cross (G.R. 344 780 and 3.5 miles from the bridge). This is a cross of 5 roads with what appears to be a disused creamery on the left. For walks 4 and 5 continue straight up to Moanflugh on the road signposted to Millstreet. Otherwise bear right on the road signposted to Ballinagree and continue for just over a mile to Carrigthomas Cross (G.R. 354 798). Turn right here for walk 3 and left for walks 6 and 8. For walk 7 continue straight to the village of Ballinagree. Details for reaching the starting point of walk 9 will be given under that walk.

3

A Circle around Cooper's Rock

This is a relatively short walk (about 5.5 miles) in the south-ernmost spur of the Boggeraghs. All of it is between the 700 and 800 ft contours and, since it is on a kind of a dry-land peninsula, it affords some really fine long-distance views to the east, south and west On one clear October afternoon we could see as far as Mangerton in Kerry to the west (25 miles) and to the east as far as the Knockmealdown mountains in Waterford (50 miles) from two different points on the walk.

Cooper's Rock (G.R: 372 776) is actually marked on the map, its height being given as 991 ft. It is a rough craggy heap of sandstone just south of Burren mountain (not named but height given as 1250 ft on the map). There is a neat well-built cairn on the summit and this makes it easily recognis-able from near and far.

Having turned right at Carrigthomas Cross you immedi-ately drive across the Laney river and the road rises steadily out of the river valley for about a mile when you come to a crossroad (G.R: 374 796). There is a good green shoulder on the road straight ahead where you can park the car. Walking back from the car to the cross take the road to the left (south).

The sharp rise ahead of you is short and, as the road levels out (temporarily), you see off ahead in the distance the conical Douce mountain in the Shehy range. Very shortly craggy Doughill appears to the right (east) of Douce and further to the right are the lofty heights above Gougane Barra and then to the left of Douce come Shehy mountain it-self and Nowen in that order thereby completing a beautiful distant prospect of the Shehy range. As your eye travels from left to right past the Shehy range you see some of the peaks of the Derrynasaggart range and of the Boggeragh range itself. If you are lucky with the day you may be able to see Mangerton mountain away in the distance behind the

39

gap between the Shehys and the Derrynasaggarts. In the immediate foreground the green fields of the Laney valley fall away southward towards Macroom. This whole beautiful backdrop is going to be with you for a few miles. Distant shapes and perspectives will change as the road meanders and as the light changes. As you stop to take your first look at the entire scene you will notice in the fields below you the remains of a stone circle – relic of a far back civilisation.

As you continue walking, Cooper's Rock itself appears on your left just three fields away and its topping cairn is clearly visible and then, just as the road swings left, in the field on your right is a pair of magnificent standing stones. Go into the field and stand between them and admire the great view to the west and to the south away across the valley of the Lee towards the heights of Templemartin and beyond even to the sea. Give a thought to the erectors of the stones. Did they see what you see and did they stop to admire it? To what extent has the scene changed from their day? Were the stones placed in this precise spot to command the entire scene? Who knows!

Back to the road which begins to fall as it crosses a little fast-flowing stream hidden in the foliage. Very shortly after crossing the stream take the road to the left and up a sharp climb. As you climb, look back at the standing stones as they in turn look towards the Derrynasaggarts, Musherabeg and Musheramore. Soon you come to a derelict stone house on your left shortly beyond which is an opening into a field. This is the best point to take off for your trip to the top of Cooper's Rock. Just go straight up following the stony path and in about 10 minutes you are there. Sit down on the pile of stones and enjoy the view, not alone the view, but also the silence, something which is becoming more and more difficult to find in today's living.

Having returned to the road turn left as you emerge from the field and go with the fall of ground to a cluster of trees, an attractive entrance and avenue on your right and a little further on a large cream-coloured house on your left. Take the road to the left immediately before this house and follow it up a fairly steep climb for about 0.5 mile until you see ahead of you a cottage (painted green at the time of writing) immediately before which is a junction left which you take. As the road rises look back at that superb view which has been with you for the last few miles, but shortly Cooper's Rock will come between you and it. At the highest point of the road where it swings left look over the rusty 6-bar gate towards the north-east and on the skyline you should make out the heights of the Knockmealdown mountains – almost 50 miles away. Ahead on the left is the rounded hump of Burren mountain and you now coast down around the side of it passing a homestead in trees. If the gate across your road is closed pass through and close it after you. Continue your way downhill, noting the forestry on your left until you join a wider road on to which you turn left walking along through the forestry on each side. Ahead you will soon see the blunt top of Mullaghanish with its relay mast. Just when you emerge from the trees and where the road begins to fall you see the green pastures of the lower slopes of Musheramore and Musherabeg with Ballinagree church nestling in their midst. This green bowl-like formation is the work of the Laney river and its many tributaries which drain the southern slopes of the Boggeraghs. The Laney flows south to join the Sullane just before the latter joins the Lee, east of Macroom town.

Enjoy the pleasant view as the road gradually falls for over a mile down to the cross where you left your car.

Distance: 5.5 miles. Time: 2.5 hours.

4

On the Southern Slopes of Musherabeg

This walk is about the same length as the round of Cooper's Rock. It does not offer similar spectacular vistas but it has a pleasant charm which is difficult to define. Broadly speaking it traverses the valley shoulders of the Cusloura river which runs down the southern slopes of Musherabeg to join the Laney. It passes through a countryside which once was densely populated – to judge by the many derelict homes to be seen along the route. To add to its charm you will meet hardly any road traffic at all and consequently, the sounds of the countryside predominate.

The starting point is Moanflugh School which is marked on the map at G.R: 324 798 and which is reached by turning left at Bawnmore Cross and driving along for about 2 miles on a gently rising road to a T junction at which the school faces you. Your best parking place is close to the wall of the school yard.

Standing with the school on your left you are facing north up the road to the col between Musherabeg and Musheramore. Notice that the road behind you runs south-west to a crossroad next to which is the mark *Gallain* and that the road to the right at this cross runs north-west to join the main Macroom–Millstreet road at Carriganimmy (more about this road later). Now with the school still on your left, walk a few yards forward (northward) to a road branching off to the left.[1] This is the road to take. It runs westward and joins the road to Carriganimmy previously referred to at a point, the G.R. of which is 306 796. It has an enticing green spine and it soon begins to rise offering good views ahead of Musherabeg and Musheramore. You pass a cluster of homes still occupied on your right while ahead you can see a crag

---

[1] This road is not marked on the earlier printings of Sheet 21.

to which the road rises. Soon you join the road leading to Carriganimmy and you turn right and continue the climb up to a pass at 900 ft. Near the pass notice on your left the ruined stone building – the remains of Carrignaspirroge (rock of the sparrow-hawks) church – a pointer to a one-time high population in the area. Just beyond the top of the pass do not take the road going to the right. It is a cul-de-sac which skirts the forestry and leads to a farmstead. But do notice the very fine stone circle in the field between the road on which you are and that going to the right (the map clearly puts it on the other side). There are 5 stones in the circle and 2 odd ones some distance from the circle. Now face north-west and admire the panorama which the erectors saw many centuries ago. Immediately below is the valley of the Keel river which divides the Boggeraghs from the Derrynasaggarts. Beyond is the gradual rise of land off towards the slopes of Mullaghanish.

At this point take a look at the map and notice the dotted short-cut road connecting the road on which you are with the one running west-east and onto which you want to get. This link is now nothing more than a muddy cattle track which skirts along the forestry. Nevertheless it can be walked and it will take off the other 2 sides of the triangle, amounting to about 0.75 mile.

Having got on to the west-east road either by the short or long route, follow the climb with the forestry on your right and rocky crags on your left. Soon you will reach the highest point just above the hairpin bend. Musherabeg is now straight ahead. On your right there is the entire expanse of the *moin fluich* – the wet flatland. This has been the work of the Cusloura (which you will soon cross) which has washed down material from the heights of Musherabeg to form a plain through which it meanders before joining the Laney, the valley of which you can see further off to the right. Further forestry now approaches on your left as you skirt around the upper end of the *moin fluich*. At this stage the road has swung north in order to 'vee-up' to cross the Cusloura by an old stone bridge after which it turns south-east. As you walk along notice all the derelict homesteads – most

43

of them set back from the road with traces of the boreens leading into them. Rough scrub has taken over where once there were fertile fields.

The road finally joins that coming down from the Musherabeg–Musheramore col. Turn right at the junction and follow the gently falling slope back to the school. Along the way you cross the Cusloura again, now much wider and more slow-moving. Look over the left-hand parapet of the bridge and you will clearly see the approaches to the ford which preceded the bridge.

Distance: 5.5 miles. Time: 2 hours.

5

Between Musherabeg and Musheramore

If you have done the previous walk and feel that it has not been long or exciting enough to justify the drive from Macroom – or more so from Cork – why not try, in addition, this very pleasant and different walk between Musherabeg and Musheramore or to give it another title, *Up and Down The Valley Shoulders of the Awboy Stream*. Its starting point is Moanflugh school but be warned, it is about 6.8 miles and if you need sustenance between the two walks there is none at Moanflugh and certainly none on the route. The nearest hostelry is about 3 miles back towards Macroom.

The Awboy is another tributary of the Laney which rises up in the col between Musherabeg and Musheramore and has carved out the valley between the two peaks. As with the Cusloura in the previous walk you will cross it twice – once up high where it is small and again lower down when it has grown considerably.

Start from the school as in the previous walk but ignore the road on the left. About 0.5 mile further on there is a road on the right which you also ignore. This is in fact the end of the walk. Another road to the left slightly further on should also be ignored (this is, of course, the return road of the previous walk). Soon the road narrows and signs of a green spine begin to appear as you pass a farmstead on the right. This is the last occupied home which you are going to see for quite a few miles. A belt of evergreens on the right affords intermittent views across the valley to Musheramore. The steadily rising road shortly comes out into open country with a fine view of Musherabeg ahead on the left, followed shortly by a splendid view of Musheramore on your right. You are looking here at two peaks – the higher one (2118 ft) being Musheramore, the other being the unnamed one of height 1856 ft. Very shortly as the road continues to rise, you

45

come into sheep country and the Awboy valley begins to narrow and ahead you can see the col between the two peaks and this is where the road is heading for on its northerly course. Now if you look carefully at the map you will see forestry marked on the left-hand side but you will notice that all that now remain are hundreds of tree stumps interspersed with boulders. You are now in real Boggeragh country where green fields have yielded to heath and moorland. After about 3 miles from the start the road begins to swing to the right (to the north-east) and continues to rise to the point where it joins the road coming up the shoulder of Musheramore.

Turn right and begin the long descent down the other shoulder of the Awboy stream but before you do so sit on the grassy bank and enjoy the magnificent panorama off to the south-west (i.e. along the line of the road on which you have just been walking). You are looking far across the valley of the young river Lee in the vicinity of Inchigeelagh towards Bantry Bay and as the eye moves more towards the south one sees the fall of land away from the Boggeraghs towards Cork city. Behind you, you will notice a road junction and a road sign. These will feature in later walks (6 and 8).

As you descend continue to enjoy that grand prospect ahead. It looks at its very best on a late sunny afternoon when the sun is in the west and lighting up the distant hills and plains. After about a mile you enter a belt of forestry and shortly you pass the first occupied house which you have seen for some miles and about 0.5 mile further on take the narrow road to the right which slopes downward. This road is easily identified by the white cottage at the junction. The road, with its green spine, soon turns south and after about a mile crosses the Awboy and immediately turns sharply right and rises abruptly past a colourful homestead on the left. Where it levels out, a road comes in on the right; ignore this; it is a cul-de-sac. Shortly you arrive at a T junction where you turn left to Moanflugh school and your car.

Distance: 6.8 miles. Time: 2.5 hours.

6

A Circle around Musheramore

This walk is over 11 miles and makes a great day's outing. It takes one through all the facets of Boggeragh country. At two points it reaches a height of 1400 ft and affords splendid vistas of near and far. Although 11 miles may appear a bit long, be encouraged by the fact that just when the legs may be beginning to tire, the final 3 miles are downhill!!

To get to the starting point drive up to Carrigthomas Cross and turn left onto a gradually rising road. Having passed through some pieces of forestry you come into open country and you get a good view ahead to the right of Musheramore around which you are about to walk. About a mile from the cross you come to a road to the right (G.R: 346 814) and this is your starting point. There is ample parking on the grassy margin at the junction.

The first 0.5 mile of this minor road runs through flat marshy land but then it begins to rise and, at the same time, swing towards the west and slowly a splendid view begins to unfold on the left which expands as you go higher passing a farmstead on your right and approaching forestry on your left. Just before entering the forestry stop and enjoy that view which is probably the finest of the entire walk although you are still well below 1,400 ft. Looking due west you see afar Shehy itself well separated from Douce on the right and further right Doughill followed by the heights of Keimaneigh and Gougane Barra and in the very far distance, some of the Kerry peaks. Going to the left of Shehy, one can see Nowen and, further away, the heights around Castle Donovan and the hinterland of Bantry Bay. Nor should you overlook the very attractive scenery closer to hand – a pleasant mix of green fields, forestry as well as scattered trees and immediately on the left Musherabeg. Just where the road turns north a road comes in on the right. This road comes up from Ballinagree and forms part of Walk 7. You will notice from your map that the road ahead takes a big loop as it crosses a number of little streams which comprise the headwaters of the Laney. This is a beautiful and quiet stretch of road with stretches of forestry on both sides but yet affording pleasing views to the right of the lower fertile slopes of the Bogger-aghs and – in the distance – of the Lee valley. About 4.2 miles from the starting point you come to a T junction where you turn left onto what is known as the Butter Road or the Kerry Road about which we shall have something to say later in the walk.

As you now begin the short sharp climb up to the col between Mushera and Seefin you very soon come into open country with a good view of the rounded top of Mushera (as distinct from Musheramore) ahead of you on the left and soon you are in the lee of it as you reach the top which is just above the 1,400 ft contour. And just as you pass the bog on your right a huge panorama to the north comes into view. This is, of course, the broad fertile valley of the Blackwater river between Millstreet and Mallow. Notice the neatly rounded hump immediately in front of you and locate it on the map. It is Claragh (1486 ft) – the easternmost peak of the Derrynasaggart range. The high land which you see in the distance beyond Claragh is the Mullaghareirk mountain range on the Kerry–Limerick border. Turning somewhat to the right you can see (if the day is clear) in the very far dis-tance the Slieve Felim mountains – 40 miles away in west Tipperary.

You are now 5 miles from the start and although the go-ing has been fairly strenuous you will agree that it has been well worth it. You may like to take a rest here which is close to the half-way point but it is generally fairly breezy up here and a more sheltered and more interesting spot about 1.5 mile down the hill is suggested. As you walk downhill con-tinue to enjoy the view ahead. By the way, not very far from the top is a well of clear water set in a neat stone surround on you left where you can slake your thirst. Slightly over a mile from the top a road comes in on the right and slightly further on also on the right, you come to a big slab of stone set in the ditch. This is the Kerryman's Table and is an appropriate spot to rest and read what follows.

Go to the bottom right-hand corner of Sheet 21 and locate the little village of Tower (G.R: 582 748) which is about 6 miles from Cork city. Notice the straight stretch (5 miles) of road running north-west therefrom then running west for 3 miles and north-west again up the side of Mushera and down the other side (where you now are) on to Millstreet. From Millstreet west to Rathmore (G.R: 174 930) it more of less coincides with the main road (R582) and then strikes away cross country for 16 miles with only a single bend to Castleisland and thence coinciding with the main road (N21) to Tralee. Time was (up to the mid-nineteenth century) when this was the trunk route serving much of Cork and Kerry and had many branches to left and right as is clear from the map. To the Corkman it was the Kerry Road; to the Kerryman it was the Butter Road. Along this road came, day after day, the vast quantities of butter made in the country homes to the great butter market in Cork city from where it was exported to many parts of the world. And it is easy to follow the road from Tower into the city, through the little village of Kerry Pike – along Blarney Road and down to the foot of Blarney Street close to where the butter market buildings were. You are sitting on the spot where the Kerrymen are said to have taken a rest before facing up the climb to Mushera followed by the long descent down to the city. Much of the route has given way to more convenient, more populated and less hilly roads. Nevertheless its entire length is surfaced (albeit a few pot-holed stretches here and there) and it makes a most scenic and interesting drive all the way from Cork to Tralee or vice versa. Incidentally, of all the possible routes between Cork and Tralee it is the shortest. The journeyman of the past did not mind the steep climb or the trek across bleak country as long as it shortened the distance.

Back on the road, continue the fall of ground down to the crossroad. Ahead of you and slightly to the left of Claragh is Caherbarnagh (2239 ft), one of the higher points of the Derrynasaggart range. At the cross turn left (signposts to St John's Well and Knocknakilla Stone Circle) and begin the 1.5

mile climb up the shoulder of Musheramore which you see on your left ahead. For quite a while you can enjoy good views (to the right) of Caherbarnagh and Mullaghanish and if you care to look back you can still see the green Blackwater valley. At the signpost on your left to St John's Well, it is worth making the very short detour to the well where a plaque explains its early pagan origins and where there is a magnificent view of the Derrynasaggarts. Resume your climb through forestry finally emerging into open country as you near the 1,400 ft summit and, as you reach it, you see that the whole scene changes as you look off down towards the south and west. The road to the right and signposted to Knocknakilla Stone Circle is the starting point of Walk 8 and if you have done Walk 5 you have been here before and are familiar with the first mile or so of the 3 mile descent towards the Laney river. The remainder of the descent is pleasant walking as you gradually enter more fertile countryside with intermittent stretches of forestry on each side. After 11.6 miles and about 4.5 hours later you arrive back to your car.

This walk is well worth repeating in the opposite direction, that is commencing by heading straight up to the Musherabeg–Musheramore col. It is quite a different experience.

Distance: 11.6 miles. Time: 4.5 hours.

7

Ballinagree and Carrigagulla

This pleasant walk is in the area immediately to the south-east of Walk 6 and has a stretch of about 3 miles in common with it. It does not go to the heights of Walk 6 and, being about 2 miles shorter, may appeal to the walker for whom Walk 6 is a bit much as it will still give some taste of the slopes of Musheramore. It is a walk which is very easy to follow on the map and, consequently, the description given here is somewhat brief.

The starting point is the village of Ballinagree (G.R: 366 808), the home of 'the bould Thady Quill' the great hero of the song of the same name. There is plenty of parking just left of the main road near the church. Take the road ascending by the side of the church and passing some new homes. On the map this road is represented by two thin lines close together and going north (with a little west) out of the village. It is a delightful road with a green spine and no traffic. After about 0.5 mile you come to a sharp bend onto a kind of a promontory. If you face west here you will see below you the winding Laney valley falling away towards the Lee and, in the distance, the three highlights of the Shehy mountains. As you continue to rise you will come across views of Musheramore and Musherabeg and further on the whole range of the Derrynasaggart swings into view. If the day is clear you should be able to see the humps of Mangerton and the conical tip of Torc, 25 miles away in Kerry.

The road continues to rise through evergreens and soon you pass the last inhabited home which you will see for about 5 miles and, as you come into open stony country, you see that entire great panorama in toto. Up here you cross the 1,200 ft contour and Musheramore is ahead of you as the road falls to meet the road coming in on the left. This, of course, is the road which forms the first leg of the previous walk (Number 6) and you turn right onto it but do note the very fine standing stone inside the gate near the junction. When you come to the end of this road where it joins the Butter Road turn right and follow the 2.75 mile descent through the townland of Carrigagulla. As you descend, notice the original great width (ditch to ditch) of the Butter Road and how only a fraction of this width is surfaced. Notice too how the homes are grouped together in clusters – as of old and also how many of them are derelict.

When you come to the junction with the signpost to Macroom turn right. Very shortly you will cross the Laney by Carrigagulla Bridge. The concrete parapets of this bridge belie its two beautiful stone arches which are set at a slight angle to each other. They are best seen by looking over the right-hand parapet. A little over a mile further on the road crosses another stone-arched bridge and if you look over the left hand side you will see two streams (tributaries of the Laney) meeting just under the arch. As you continue on towards Ballinagree you will enjoy the good views of the Laney away below you on the left and beyond the rounded heights of Burren mountain.

Distance: 9.5 miles. Time: 3–4 hours.

8

On the Northern Slopes of the Boggeraghs or a Circle around the Upper Reaches of the Owenbaun River

Whereas the previous Boggeragh walks have been on the southern slopes of the range, this one explores some of the northern slopes. It is a 7 mile round of the upper valley of the Owenbaun River, a tributary of the Blackwater which it joins just north of the village of Rathcool. It is not the most spectacular of the Boggeragh walks but it is a very enjoyable one and ideal for a lazy summer day and, for an added bonus, it has on its route a magnificent stone circle. On Walks 5 and 6 when you were up at the col between Musheramore and Musherabeg (G.R: 318 848) you will have noticed the beckoning road running westward and carrying a signpost to Knocknakilla Stone Circle. Your starting point is here at the junction and there is ample parking space on the grassy margins nearby.

Take to the Knocknakilla road which, after a level start, soon begins to fall and affords extensive views of the upper regions of the Owenbaun on your right while on your left the northern face of Musherabeg towers above you. After about 1.5 mile you will see forestry ahead but shortly before the road enters it notice, on your left, the exceptionally fine stone circle of Knocknakilla (hill of the wood) – five small stones forming the circle and one very tall leaning one. It is well worth going into the field and standing within the circle to appreciate the very extensive view (to the west and north) from this commanding position. Incidentally the map places the circle on the other side of the road!!!

Back on the road, continue through the forestry and turn sharp right at the junction and follow an interesting road with an exceptionally large variety of deciduous trees on both sides and fine views of Musheramore to the south (right). In the broad basin between you and Musheramore you will see roads and tracks here and there, some of them leading to homesteads, others into turf-cutting areas. Do not be tempted to consider making for one of them by way of a short cut. They are all cul-de-sacs so maintain your course but do notice an interesting landmark on the far side of the basin in the form of a narrow grove of coniferous trees in the shape of L. It is clearly marked on the map and you will pass by it in due course. It obviously at some stage provided a shelter belt but for what?

Shortly you will pass a road coming in on your left and a short distance further on a road comes in on your right (derelict house at junction). Do not take this turn. It is a 2 mile long cul-de-sac. Keep on straight for about another 0.5 mile and enjoy the scenery of the eastern end of the Derryna-saggarts – round, symmetrical Claragh on your left ahead with towering Caherbarnagh behind. Now turn right up a short rise and along a straight stretch of about 1 mile to (according to the map) Lackdotia House surrounded by trees. About 0.5 mile further on you cross the L-shaped grove already mentioned. The road now falls rapidly to cross the Owenbaun river and then rises again and is joined by a narrow road coming in on the left. This road is not on the map although the houses along its line are clearly marked!! A concrete road going off to the right is not on the map either!! Ignore both of these, keeping to the badly-surfaced steep climb ahead which rises more than 300 ft in less than 0.5 mile. However, there are plenty of boulders along the way on which to sit and get your wind and enjoy the panorama to the north.

Soon you will join the road going up by St John's Well (Walk 6) to the col from which you started.

Distance: 7 miles. Time: 2.5 hours.

9

Around the Periphery of Glannaharee Wood

For our final walk in Boggeragh country we go to its eastern extremity, to a somewhat different terrain and very definitely different vistas due to the fact that the country here is open to the north-east and east. Furthermore, for the most of its 10.5 miles it goes through deserted countryside and hence there is even less vehicular traffic to disturb you.

In order to identify the starting point on the map let us first identify the wood. The G.R. of its mid-point is 450 880 and, as you see, the map does not name it as such but the name Glannaharee appears in its north-west corner on what is labelled French's Road. Having located the wood and French's Road on the map run your finger eastward along French's Road taking the sharp right-hand bend at the road junction and follow the road south down to the first junction right. This is your starting (and finishing) point and its G.R. is 476 852. Notice that it is about half-way between Gowlane North and Gowlane South on a road which terminates at its junction with the main Coachford–Mallow road (R619). This will help you to find the starting point easily whether you are approaching it from Macroom or Cork. If you are coming from Macroom take R618 to Coachford village where you turn left onto R619 at the signpost to Mallow. This road climbs steadily up to Donoughmore and then falls sharply down to the Shournagh River at a hamlet called New Tipperary (not marked on the map) where it turns left, then right and after about 0.5 mile right again. There is a signpost here to Bweeng and Mallow but instead of turning right continue straight ahead on the narrow road for a mile to the starting point. If you are coming from Cork take N22 to the western end of the Carrigrohane Straight Road where you turn right on to R579 which you follow through Cloghroe up to

Crean's Cross Roads (marked on map). Turn right at the signpost to Donoughmore thereby joining the R619 from Coachford and continuing on to Donoughmore and beyond as described above. Whether you are coming from Macroom or Cork you have a very attractive drive of less than 20 miles with good scenery especially when you reach the Crean's Cross Roads and Donoughmore area which is 700 ft up. In fact this is a case where getting there adds appreciably to the total pleasure. The road up from the junction with R619 is narrow but there are plenty of spots near the starting point where it is wide enough to enable you to park close to the ditch.

Strike off along the road ahead of you. It is a superb walking road and in about 3 miles rises from 500 to over 1,000 ft and never steeply enough to make it an effort. There are a few homesteads along the first mile or so. Fertile fields on your right give way to barren slopes, cut here and there by deep valleys carrying streams to the Shournagh river. Beyond the fields there is a vast expanse of falling country towards the east and off in the distance the Nagle mountains (near Mallow) look quite low while further still off in the north-east you can see the Galtee mountains of south Tipperary (about 30 miles from you). There are quite a few gates along the right-hand side of the road which form convenient viewing points. The green fields in due course give way to coniferous forestry and as you continue to rise, you will see tree-clad Bweeng Mountain (1372 ft) with its telecommunication mast at the top. Just where the road swings westwards the road up from Bweeng village joins on the right but you continue along French's Road. Nobody seems to know who French was (a local landlord?) but the road would appear to be quite old – to judge by its great width (only the central spine is surfaced).

Not too far beyond the junction you cross the 1,100 ft contour which is a watershed between south and north. All the streams that you have seen and crossed so far flow down to the Shournagh which joins the Lee at Leemount – a few miles west of Cork city and those which lie ahead of you join the Glen river which joins the Blackwater at Banteer. As the

56

road ahead falls it closely follows the course of the Glen river high above its northern bank. All the while Glannaharee wood has been on your left and now on the other side of the watershed it is still with you but across the Glen river. As the road continues to fall you get occasional glimpses of the summit of Musheramore ahead of you slightly to the left.

Ultimately you will see on the left ahead down in the valley a narrow straight road which rises up out of the valley and runs south-east by the side of Glannaharee wood. This is the road for you. Now look at the map and identify this road. You will see that it takes off from the Cork–Kanturk road (R579) about half a mile south of the junction with French's Road. Traces of roads down in the valley may tempt you to take a short-cut from where you are to the road to which you wish to get but do not be tempted. Continue on the falling French's Road, crossing two streams and eventually joining R579 where you turn left. This is a reasonably busy road but then you are on it for less than 0.5 mile when you turn left onto the falling narrow road. This has a green spine. It crosses innumerable streams and after almost a mile rises fairly abruptly and you soon meet Glannaharee Wood on your left. Just around here you may notice on your right an ancient stone structure. It looks vaguely like part of a promontory fort but there is no reference to it on any map or in any work on local archaeological sites.

Continue the gradual climb for about 2 miles with forestry on each side up into open moorland at 1,100 ft This is really bleak and empty countryside. After another mile notice the surfaced road coming in on the right. This is not marked on the map and by the fact that there is not a trace of habitation on it as far as one can see suggests that it may have been a 'turf-road'. Up here there are extensive areas of turf bog and huge quantities of turf were harvested during the Second World War to keep Cork city warm and many roads were built into the bogs to facilitate transport.

Shortly after the junction with the 'turf road' the road begins to fall having crossed the highest point and the whole scene suddenly changes as the land falls to the south and east and a great vista lies before you. You are, in fact looking off to the south coast somewhere in the direction of Bally-cotton – Youghal – Ardmore. As you continue to descend (keeping straight ahead at a staggered crossroads) away to your left the Nagles and the Galtees appear again. Coming down here one sunny June evening about 7 o'clock was an unforgettable experience as the mighty landscape far and near was lit by a westering sun.

Continuing your descent you come to a Y junction where you take the left arm. You are now well and truly back in 'civilisation' as the fertile land hereabouts is well populated. Continue the gradual descent until you join the road on which you left your car.

Distance: 10.5 miles. Time: about 4 hours.

The Derrynasaggart Mountains

The Derrynasaggarts are the western neighbours of the Boggeraghs (Sheet 21), the Macroom–Millstreet road (R582) forming their eastern boundary. On the north they may be regarded as bounded by a line from Millstreet north-west to Rathmore (G.R: 174 930) and thence south-west to Barraduff (G.R: 088 904). Their western boundary is less clearly definable as they merge almost unbroken into the Shehy mountains which lie to their south-west. For convenience and clarity we shall set an arbitrary western boundary as a line from Barraduff south to Morley's Bridge (G.R: 048 750). Here our boundary line turns south to Ballingeary which is just off the lower edge of Sheet 21 but the G.R. of which is 150 670. The last side of this rather irregular hexagon runs from Ballingeary eastward to Macroom.

The Derrynasaggarts straddle the boundary line between the counties of Kerry and Cork. A look at the black dotted boundary line on the map will certainly raise the question: Who decided on such a crazy, irregular boundary? A closer look may provide an answer in that the dividing line goes all the way through high (uninhabitable) land thus avoiding villages, communities and farmland. The Derrynasaggarts also contain higher and more easily identifiable peaks than the Boggeraghs, for example rounded Claragh in the east, flat-topped Mullaghanish (with its T.V./Radio relay mast) and of course the twin highest peaks – the Paps. If you drive from Macroom to Killarney on the main road (N22) just beyond the highest point at what is known as 'The County Bounds' (G.R: 140 804) the Paps face you straight ahead and you will understand how apt is their name!!

Derrynasaggart country is considerably different from that of the Boggeraghs. It is somewhat 'softer' although on the average, it is higher. The land is more fertile but the

peaks are still very bleak. The density of roads is considerably less although the population is probably higher and there are far less relics of the past – both distant and immediate. The lower mileage of roads inevitably leads to less walks and not too many suitable circular walks come to light. Furthermore the eastern slopes are almost entirely under forestry and this does not make for interesting walking in that area.

The routes of all the walks are completely within the limits of Sheet 21 and all map references in the text are to this sheet unless otherwise stated. Furthermore since all grid references are in the W Sub-Zone the letter W will be omitted where these are quoted.

10
Dundareirke, Kilnamartyra and beyond

Dundareirke is an anglicised version of the Irish: Dun da Radharc – fort of two views. The name appears on the map (G.R: 302 716) in Gothic script to indicate the ruined castle of that name. To enjoy the two views simultaneously over a stretch of about 3 miles it is suggested that you defer visiting the castle (what is left of it) until close to the end of the walk.

Your starting point (see, however, note at end of walk) is at the crossroad a short distance to the south of the castle. If you are starting from Macroom turn off the main street up towards the Catholic church and bear right immediately beyond it. Shortly after the 'end-of-speed-limit' sign bear right at the fork and continue straight ahead for about 2 miles until you come to another fork (at which there is a signpost to Macroom). Bear right here and after about 0.5 mile you arrive at the crossroad starting point. Your walk goes straight ahead and you can park with safety close to the cemetery wall.

If you are coming from Cork it may be more convenient to take the Macroom–Inchigeelagh road (R584) from its junction with the main Cork–Macroom road (N22). This junction is about 0.25 mile east of Macroom. Continue on the R584 until you come to the western end of the Geragh (see below) shortly after which there is a turn to the right (G.R: 302 708). Immediately after you turn right you will notice another road going to the right. Avoid this and stay with the one that goes steeply up the hill and in less than 0.5 mile you will reach the crossroad referred to above where you turn left.

The cemetery is an old one and commands a grand view to the south (of little benefit to these lying within!!) over the Lee valley to the heights of Teerelton and Cappeen. Immediately below you is Toon Bridge which carries the Macroom–

63

Inchigeelagh road over the Toon river which joins the Lee at the western end of the Geragh, that wide expanse of water created in the1950s for hydro-electricity purposes. Notice, by the way, that the cemetery gate has an arch. This is a feature (the lich) which is quite common in England but relatively rare in Ireland.

The road on which you are about to walk westward is a 'ridge' road that is, it runs along the spine of what one might call an 'inland peninsula'. In this case the 'peninsula' runs east-west and since there is falling land on each side (i.e. south and north) the road commands extensive views in both of these directions and indeed also towards the west. Yet for the first 0.5 mile or so there is little to see until you pass the old school on the left and then quite suddenly the view to the north opens up revealing some of the main peaks of the Derrynasaggarts–Mullaghanish with its TV/Radio mast and the Paps off to the west. Immediately below is the fertile valley of the Sullane river. A few yards further on the view to the south and west suddenly springs open revealing the whole range of the Shehy mountains. Moving from right to left there is the sloping ridge of Mweelin (really part of the Derrynasaggarts) followed by the sharp bluff of Coomataggart on the Cork–Kerry border and then by three of the four landmarks of the Shehys – craggy Doughill, cone-shaped Douce and Shehy mountain itself. Incidentally the Shehys are too far south to be on Sheet 21. You must go to the West Cork sheet (24) for them. Of course if you have with you the Ireland South sheet you will have both views fully mapped.

The road now falls somewhat to a crossroad (only the left arm is shown on the map) with an impressive standing stone in the field on the western side of the byroad. This is the first of three spread over a mile westward and forming a straight line. At this stage you are considerably 'closer' to the view ahead and Nowen Hill, the fourth landmark of the Shehys has begun to show its peak. After about another 0.5 mile you come to an unsurfaced road going south immediately to the west of which is the second standing stone. The road rises again and within the next 0.5 mile reaches its highest point. Here, opposite an unsurfaced road to the left, is the third of the standing stones and here too you have an absolutely unobstructed panoramic view through almost 180 degrees. Notice away in the far distance to the left of the Paps how Mangerton mountain in Kerry stands out.

Immediately below you is the village of Kilnamartyra. Walk down to the village and turn right immediately after passing the church at the signpost to Macroom. As you descend to the valley of the Sullane you have a very fine view to your left of its upper reaches towards the County Bounds. Straight ahead of you stands Mullaghanish while somewhat to your right is Musheramore. After about 0.75 mile the road levels out and swings sharply left. At this point take the narrow road on the right which runs due east for about 2 miles to your next turning point. There is little to be said about this low-lying monotonous stretch except that in high summer it is pleasantly shaded by a superb variety of trees.

Keep going until you meet a surfaced road on the right which you take. This has a nice green spine and climbs steadily up to Dundareirke through dense woodland. After about 0.75 mile the road levels out and you will see on your left the remaining corner of Dundareirke castle. It is well worth climbing over the ditch and walking out along the promontory on which the ruin stands and enjoying the great view of which Charles Smith in his *Ancient and Present State of the County and City of Cork* published in 1815, wrote 'The Castle of Dundarerke (*sic*) which signifies Mount Prospect is seated on a hill – and commands a vast extended view to the west as far as the bounds of Kerry; to the east almost to Cork and a great tract to the south'.

Rejoin the road and continue south to the crossroad whence you started and enjoy the vista ahead of you across the Toon and Lee valleys.

Distance : 7 miles. Time : about 2.5 hours.

Doing this walk in reverse is not recommended as the great views on the ridge road will be behind you.

Beyond Kilnamartyra

If you have become 'hooked' on the ridge road and all that you can see from it you can continue on it beyond Kilnamartyra by turning left instead of right in the village. It holds its height and attendant views for another 2 miles before it begins to fall into forestry. At Cloontycarty (G.R: 206 716) take the sharp left turn onto the road which follows the valley of the Toon eastward to Toon Bridge. Parts of this road are attractive but much of it is rather monotonous and the whole is a 6 mile trek. However as you can see from the map you can shorten this trek by taking either of the two left turns off the ridge road and thereby striking the Toon valley road closer to Toon Bridge.

If you consider exploring beyond Kilnamartyra, as indicated above, it may be more convenient at the outset to leave the car at Toon Bridge (plenty of parking space on the south side next to the shop), to walk back over the bridge turning right and then after about 0.5 mile turning left and up the sharp climb to Dundareirke.

11
Beyond Ballyvourney Towards the County Bounds

The village of Ballyvourney (G.R.: 194 776) is on the Cork–Macroom–Killarney road (N22) at the point where the road begins its climb up over the Derrynasaggart mountains to the Cork–Kerry border (the County Bounds) followed by its fall along the shoulder of the Clydagh valley (Walk 12) into Kerry. This walk takes you from the village through rising land towards the County Bounds and back again and yet placing you for only about 1 mile on the busy N22. There are no great spectacular vistas but the countryside is broad, open and varied and the roads are virtually devoid of traffic.

The route of the walk becomes clear when looked at on the map. Therefore locate Ballyvourney. Notice a road going off the main road to the left immediately beyond the river (not before it; the road before the river goes up to Coolea) and call this road A. Notice a very minor road B joining A from the north-west and at its other end leaving the main road. Notice also a second-class road, C roughly parallel with B also leaving the main road and running south-east-ward and joining up with A about 1.5 mile further west. The walk consists of going west on A to its junction with C and following C until it joins the main road on which you walk eastward to the junction with B and following B back to A. The car can be parked in the village.

Very shortly after leaving the village on the main road (towards Kerry) take the left-hand turn into the narrow tree-lined road which falls a little at first, passes some new homes on the right and, after about 0.5 mile, is joined by road B on the right. Continue walking along road A in a south-wester-ly direction. The road becomes even narrower and undulates quite a lot but affords good views of Coolea and the Sullane valley to the left and of the heights of Coom ahead. In less than 1.5 mile it begins to rise gradually and after another 0.5 mile you come to a crossroad where a surfaced road goes to the left and an unsurfaced road goes to the right and the road on which you are swings right and turns away from the Sullane valley and onto the shoulder of the valley of the Aughboy stream. Soon you come out in open, semi-moorland country and ahead are the heights of the County Bounds including the clearly defined 'dip' through which the N22 passes from Cork into Kerry. Very gradually the road swings from a northerly to a westerly direction. You cross a little stream where there is a weir almost exactly under the bridge. You pass the occasional farmstead on the left as you continue to rise and after about 4.5 miles from the start you arrive at the main road onto which you turn right.

There is no doubt that you are going to meet traffic at all times on this road but you will be on it for less than a mile – at the most 20 minutes. However, once you reach the unsurfaced road C on your right all will be quiet again as you walk along the 900 ft contour for about 2 miles with moorland on each side of you and a pleasant vista ahead. The road begins to fall quite steeply and passes a few deserted homesteads before the final fall to the junction with road A where you turn left and retrace your steps to the village.

Distance: 7.5 miles. Time: 2.5 hours.

A Variation: Looking at the map, specifically at the point where road B connects with the main road (G.R: 164 796) notice that there is a continuation of B on the other side of the main road which goes up close to Lake Carrignafiurark before swinging south and ultimately joining the main road down closer to the village. Much of this road has practically disappeared but its bed can be followed and provides a very fine alternative to taking road C. The continuation of B referred to above soon deteriorates to a mere track but it can be followed close up to the lake. The upland here is turf-cutting country but the cutters from the village come up from the other end of the old road which is a stony track.

When you get up near the lake you may have to look

around a little for the way forward but you should have little difficulty in spotting tractor/car tyre marks which will guide you downward to the stony track. There is no fear whatever of getting lost as you are up high and can always see the general way downward ahead and you will have had a superb walk.

To incorporate this variation in a circular walk it is suggested that you follow roads A and B as described above, cross the main road and onto the track. This will give a total distance of about 8.5 miles. There is however one snag, namely having joined the main road you have almost a mile stretch back to the village.

12
Clydagh Country

When you drive on the N22 over the County Bounds into Kerry, the road descends for about 5 miles along the southern shoulder of the valley of the Clydagh river which rises on the slopes of Caherbarnagh deep in the Derrynasaggarts and tumbles down beneath Poulgorm Bridge and on to Kenmare Bay. Except for the first few miles the Clydagh is entirely in Co. Kerry so that the cluster of walks described here is not in Cork but close enough to it to justify its inclusion.

To reach your starting point drive along N22 from Ballyvourney up over the County Bounds into Kerry. As you begin the descent notice the Paps facing you ahead and on their right two peaks marked 1958 and 1742 on the map, the latter being labelled Knocknabro. It is along the foot of these mountains that the walks mainly lie. About a mile down from the Cork–Kerry border there is, on the left, a fairly substantial derelict house which (at the time of writing) has on its gable a commercial for someone's woollen mills. Notice the road going off to the right opposite the house. This is the road back in the circular walk described in Part 1. The G.R. is 130 818.

Part 1. Both Sides of the Clydagh

There is ample parking space off the main road at the derelict house. The first 1.5 mile of the walk is down the main road. Do not let the possibility of heavy traffic put you off. For the most part the road is wide and walking is not too unpleasant being compensated for by fine views of the Paps and Rodger's Rock across the Clydagh valley and later Crohane off ahead of you. Just after passing the restaurant on your right you can get off the main road for a while by following the bed of the (unfinished) new road on the right of the existing road. Whenever Kerry County Council gets around to finishing the new road then you will be able to dodge the traffic by using what will then be the old road. As you continue the descent notice the line of houses on the other side of the valley. These lie on the road along which you will walk and for convenience we shall name it The Clydagh Road.

Very shortly before Clonkeen church and school you will see your turn to the right (G.R: 114 826). This is the beginning of the Clydagh Road which, for over 6 miles, runs eastward deeply into the Derrynasaggarts. It is a very narrow road with very little traffic even though there are quite a few homesteads on it.

Immediately after leaving the main road you cross the Clydagh river. Even in dry weather there is always a forceful flow of water but after a spell of rain it can be quite spectacular, even fearful, racing through its deep gorge. The road soon swings eastward to the right (a byroad on the left leads to a group of homesteads) and starts to rise gradually. Along here the views are pleasant rather than exciting. As you come in line with the restaurant on the main road you will notice the hump of Knockacommeen (1,408 ft) behind it. Some distance further on a surfaced road goes off to the left. This is a cul-de-sac. As the road continues to rise it tends to diverge from the main road on the other side of the valley and moves into more rugged and more scenic country with good views ahead of the Paps and the peaks to the east of them. Road and river have become more or less level with each other as you approach a bridge ahead of you on the right. This point is just about 2.5 miles from Clonkeen where you left the main road.

Having turned right you notice that you cross two bridges close together, the first over a little stream and the second over the Clydagh. After the bridges you will see a road going off to the left. This obviously serves (or served) a few homesteads along the south bank of the Clydagh and one can see its line extending eastward for quite some distance. This road is not shown on the map nor is the one coming down from the heights and joining it (this is most likely a 'turf road'). Beyond the bridge your road swings right and for a while runs level with the river. It was once surfaced but it now has a lot of loose stones and a lush green spine and it is flanked by lots of rowan trees. Soon it begins to rise up above the Clydagh and veers towards the south. After a short sharp rise you see the main road away ahead of you and after a further mile of very pleasant undulating tree-lined road you join the main road at your car.

Distance: almost 6 miles. Time: about 2 hours.

Part 2. The Entire Length of the Clydagh Road

The first 2.5 miles of the Clydagh Road have been traversed in Part 1. If you have enjoyed it you may be tempted to traverse the remaining 3.5 miles deep into the Derryna-saggarts. Unfortunately you will have to retrace your steps as, at the time of writing, there is no apparent circle. Nevertheless, the return trip is crowded with a host of views entirely different from those encountered on the way up. The Clydagh Road is a good example of a 'shoulder' road that is one which follows a river high above it on one side of its valley. In contrast to roads which run close to rivers, 'shoulder' roads being high up afford much better views of the rivers they follow and also of the countryside above and beyond the valleys.

If you wish to walk the entire length of the road it would be as well to leave your car at Clonkeen church where there is ample parking. On the other hand, if you have already done Part 1 it would be as well to drive the first 2.5 miles up to the turn right at the two bridges. There is parking close to the sheep pens.

Less than a mile beyond the turn right an unsurfaced track with a gate across it takes off to the north (left). This track forms the mainstay of the walk described in Part 3. The road now levels out and the surface begins to deteriorate and ahead on your right Mullaganish (identified by its TV mast) appears and soon on your left you pass 'Knocknabro National School 1909' now no longer in use as a school.

One's immediate reaction is 'What a place for a school!' but when one looks at the large number of homesteads, most of them now deserted, on both sides of the river one realises the large population that was once sustained by the fertile inches along by the river. The tillage is gone and sheep have taken over in the valley as well as on the more barren slopes. As you continue along the sheep become more and more plentiful and forestry begins to take over the landscape – young timber on the right of the river and that which is more mature on the left.

Soon, after a gentle climb, the road falls fairly steeply down to a new bridge on the right. This is forestry property, and is at present closed to the public. Its rather massive construction gives a good idea of the force of the Clydagh when in flood. There is a steady climb up from the bridge and the forestry soon gives way to more open country with the occasional green field hemmed in by stone walls. Soon you will pass on your right the last inhabited house and opposite it, literally in the middle of a field, a gate between two posts!! A short sharp rise in the now unsurfaced road brings a very fine vista ahead. From here on there are 2 or 3 gates across the road, their purpose being to contain sheep. They are not locked but do not forget to close them after you pass through. After a gentle climb you come to the remains of a fairly extensive homestead still used by the sheep farmers for storage purposes. The road now becomes a green track and falls down along the bank of the Clydagh to a very substantial residence with garden gone wild and outhouses beginning to crumble but the green fields on the bank of the river are still being used to grow pasture crops.

This would appear to be the end of the line although there are traces of a track going up the rocky hillside on the left of the house. This is a strange, lonely but beautiful place. The Clydagh here is relatively slow-moving. The sound of its quiet flow, the songs of the birds and the occasional 'bah' of a sheep are the pleasant intruders on the absolute peace of the scene.

Do not let the fact that you have to retrace your footsteps depress you. The return walk is almost like a new one with different vistas and different colours. You get a new slant on the Paps and here and there you catch glimpses of the more distant Kerry mountains.

Incidentally, as you walk along by the old school-house you cannot but notice the line of a road on the southern side of the valley. It is difficult to judge how much of it is old and how much new (for forestry purposes). Certainly the western end of it is old – to judge from the number of ruins. In addition there are a few roads coming down to it from the heights above. These are probably 'turf roads'. Does this road on the southern side now run from the new bridge west to the bridge near the sheep pens referred to in Part 1? If it does then there is the possibility of another circle walk in Clydagh country.

Having arrived back at Clonkeen, somewhat foot-sore perhaps, you may be inclined to say, 'I could have driven all the way to within 0.5 mile of the end and back'. This is perfectly true but you would have missed much through having to keep your eye on the narrow and ever winding road.

Distance (one way) from Clonkeen to the end of the road: 6.8 mile. Time: 2.5 hours.

Part 3. The Way to 'The City'

The title of this walk (which unfortunately is not a circle walk) is calculated to arouse your curiosity as to the whereabouts of a city amidst the Derrynasaggart mountains. If you look on your map at the northern slopes of the higher (2284 ft) of the two Paps at a point of G.R.: 140 882 you will see, in Gothic script, 'Penitential Station'. This was the title given by the surveyor of the last century to what is known far and wide in the broad Blackwater valley as 'The City'. In the Christian era it has been a place of prayer and penance for many centuries but it pre-dates Christianity by many years. It is (or was) in fact a ring fort situated at a very strategic point. (Lat. *castrum*=fort, *castra*=fortified camp. In Irish *castrum/castra* became *cathair* and later used as a translation for city.)

The way to 'The City' starts on the Clydagh Road at the point about 3.4 miles up from Clonkeen where the unsurfaced road (referred to in Part 2) takes off to the north (G.R: 140 840). It is a superb 5 mile walk, much of it on an unsurfaced track with a few gates across it and it rises to a height of 1500 ft. It is shown as a dotted line on the map. It is not suitable for cars.

A word of warning before setting out on this walk: be sure of the weather. There is no shelter of any kind for miles and close proximity to mountains can mean rain while there is sunshine at lower levels. A May day with blue skies and the odd white cloud with no haze is best. There is ample parking on the grassy verge of the Clydagh Road just where your track takes off northward (there is a modern home close to the junction).

Pass through the gateway and commence the stony climb up between the two heights of 2,284 ft (on your left) and 1,958 ft (on your right). As you go higher these heights will begin to tower over you and in just over a mile you reach the highest point with the lake of Glannafreaghaun (the Glen of the Crows or Heather) on your left ahead. As you come out of the pass and leave the peaks behind you the wide valley of the Blackwater (here running north-south between Ballydesmond and Rathmore) begins to broaden before you as you descend. Soon you pass an occasional homestead where the land is more fertile; the road widens somewhat and becomes surfaced and finally, after about 3 miles from the start, you join a road running east-west where you turn left. The next mile is rather dull and flat after what you have trod but there are better things to come. Ultimately you come to a crossroad in the neighbourhood of which are a few houses, a school and a fairly new church. This is the hamlet of Shrone – overlooked by the surveyors since it is not marked on the map although the school is. Turn left at the cross and ascend the stony road to 'The City'.

The circle is quite impressive both in its diameter and the height of its ramparts. In spite of some nearby farm buildings one gets the feeling of being in a place of onetime great importance. It is perched on a kind of promontory with

75

the Paps towering above it and that great majestic view to the west – the Macgillycuddy's Reeks on the left and the Slievemish range of the Dingle peninsula to the right.

Distance (one way): 5 miles: Time 2.5 hours.

One might say 'a fitting end to a splendid walk' – except for the trek back to the car. But maybe you could arrange to be dropped at the southern end of the walk or even at Clonkeen and collected some hours later at Shrone. The drive from Clonkeen to Shrone is clear from the map – N22 to Glenflesk followed by R570 to Barraduff where you turn right onto N72 and then right again at the signposted byroad (G.R: 126 916) to Shrone. To return to Macroom/Cork return from Shrone to N72 where you turn right for Rathmore whence you follow the R582 to Macroom via Millstreet.
Distance Clonkeen to Shrone: 13 miles.

The three walks in Clydagh Country described above are just 'pointers' to a very scenic and interesting area. You should be prepared to try various combinations of them.

13

Lackabaun

Lackabaun means 'white hillside' and there are quite a few Lackabauns in West Cork and Kerry. The one to which reference is made here has a G.R.: 098 709. It is marked on the map lying on a very minor road (much of it now a mere track but one time of considerable importance) which runs from the upper reaches of the Bunsheelin river on the Co. Cork side to the valley of the Roughty river on the Kerry side and crosses the Cork–Kerry border at 1500 ft.

The walk about to be described and which traverses this old road is the finest in the book. Over its entire 15 miles it is full of highlights, the greatest of them being Lackabaun itself – hence its title, although one could easily think of titles more descriptive and more apt. It is a long walk but on the route there is 'The Highest Pub in Ireland' where one can rest and partake of refreshment. Furthermore it is a walk well worth doing in the direction opposite to that described here. It is only when you have done it in both directions that you will really appreciate its grandeur. It is suggested however that for the first time you adopt the direction described.

To reach the starting point leave Macroom on the Killarney road (N22) and after about 5 miles take the road to the left at 'The Halfway House' and keep going (rising all the while) up to the 'Mouth of the Glen' – a distance of a little over 8 miles. The Mouth of the Glen is not marked on the map. Its G.R. is 158 710 and it is a gap in the rocky ridge which forms the watershed between the Toon and Bunsheelin rivers both of which are tributaries of the Lee river. The 8 mile run up to the Mouth of the Glen is not without its own attractions. After the first 2 miles of level ground (notice the tower of Kilnamatyra church of Walk 10 on the heights to the left) the road rises and affords very fine views off to the left of the Shehy mountains. Having skirted the little village of Reananerree the road continues to rise up the side of the large basin drained by the Toon river. It is worth stopping just before you go through the gap (there is space enough to drive in off the roadway) and casting an eye back on your left to the huge landscape which falls away from you towards the south-east.

Immediately on the other side of the gap the somewhat smaller but far the more attractive basin of the Bunsheelin greets you where a road goes off to the right signposted to Kenmare. This road is your way back but continue downhill on the principal road for about 0.5 miles to a road junction to the right (shown as a crossroad on the map). This narrow road to the right is your starting point and there is ample parking near the big gate which gives access to a road-dressing depot of the County Council. The principal road continues on downhill to Ballingeary (just off the map).

As you strike off along the narrow road cast your eye ahead out across that beautifully fertile basin or bowl surrounded by high hills. The basin is the work of the Bunsheelin river and its many little tributaries which flow down from the heights and which over many years have brought down to the lower reaches what is now the fertile soil. The Bunsheelin is the first major tributary of the young river Lee which it joins in Ballingeary village. High up on your right is Mweelin mountain (1605 ft) and as your eye swings left you see a dip or cut in the heights. This is Lackabaun – your first destination and, as your eye goes on further, you encounter the heights above Gougane Barra. Enjoy the panorama as the road maintains its height along the rim of the basin for a mile or so. In the meantime the three 'sentinels' of the Shehy range, Doughill, Douce and Shehy itself have come into view on your left. The road now begins to fall down into the basin. After about 1.3 mile from the start you come to a T junction where you turn left and continue the fall passing a number of neat and well-painted homes. Here and there still narrower roads take off to left and right all of them going to homesteads. After about 2 miles from the start, you are down in the flat of the basin where you go straight through at a crossroad and carry on to a T junction where you turn right onto the road that runs deep into the basin and keeps close to the Bunsheelin which is flanked by some beautifully green pasture. Since there are quite a few homesteads along this road you may meet a little car traffic but it is never enough to take from the quiet of this delightful road.

On the way you will pass a road going left and sign-posted to Gougane Barra. This road forms part of Walk 16. Continue on the road marked cul-de-sac and soon you will see ahead of you the heights of Lackabaun and the line of the old track running upwards. The road now becomes narrow-er and the green spine becomes more pronounced as the sides of the basin begin to close in. Shortly before you come to a large shed on the right with a lot of farm machinery around it a surfaced road takes off to the right. This will form part of the next walk. Finally at a buff-coloured cottage the road divides into two grassy tracks. This point is 4 miles from your car.

The right-hand grassy track is the one for you and per-haps from where you stand it seems quite formidable since it appears to climb almost vertically to the heights above. True enough you have to rise by about 700 ft in a mile or so but there is no danger whatsoever. This is not a mere sheep track but the remains of a main road. Taylor and Skinner's *Maps of the Roads of Ireland*, published in 1778 indicates it as the route from Inchigeelagh and the upper Lee valley to Ken-mare Bay. As you climb you will see evidence of this here and there where the original stonework of the foundations has been exposed by rain and wind over many years. As you ascend do not forget to cast the occasional eye back to admire the great view of the Bunsheelin basin receding from you and the Lee valley appearing off to the south.

At the top the track levels out and passes between crags on each side. For a memorable experience scramble up to the top of the crag on your left. Here you have a view to the east almost as far as Cork city and to the west away into the heart of the Kerry mountains. This is one of those places where it is good to be – there is sunshine, scenery, silence (except for the whine of the breeze in the rough tall grass) and solitude.

Back on the track you pass one or two gates and then you begin the descent down the length of the valley of the

Roughty river. The going here is somewhat stony as you traverse open moorland but well within a mile of the summit the track becomes a narrow surfaced road as you approach a homestead no longer inhabited. The next 2 miles wind downward nice and gradually with the green pasture of the valley on your left and here and there glimpses of the Kerry mountains ahead. Not far beyond the uninhabited homestead referred to above there is a strange stone structure on the left next to the road. It is well constructed with an entrance the sides of which converge on each other and terminate at the back in flat stones. In fact less the 0.5 mile further on there is another such structure – also on the left. As the road continues to fall, trees, both coniferous and deciduous become more frequent and the landscape softer and in less than 3 miles from the summit you approach a T junction where you turn right onto the road between Coolea and Morley's Bridge. Some distance before the T junction you will notice that the Roughty has swung away westward from the road on its way to Morley's Bridge where it joins the Clydagh (of Walk 12).

You now begin the gradual climb of about 1.5 mile up to what is known as 'The Top of Coom'. You are likely to meet some traffic on this stretch, nevertheless you can still enjoy this pleasant road as it soon comes out into open and rather barren county. It runs along the shoulder of a little shallow valley carved out by a stream which rises in the heights near Coom and ultimately joins the Roughty. As you climb towards the top cast an eye backward now and again to enjoy splendid views of the Kerry mountains.

Just before you reach the summit you arrive at 'The Highest Pub in Ireland' (1,000 ft). You have now walked 9.5 miles and perhaps a rest and a refreshment are in order. Just beyond the pub you cross from Kerry back into Cork and there straight ahead of you are the familiar masted landmark of Mullaghanish and surrounding heights of the Derrynasaggarts. Bear right at the junction (the road to the left descends to Coolea and Ballyvourney) on a narrow road which maintains its height (about 900 ft) for its entire 5.5 miles south-westward to the Mouth of the Glen.

This is a superb road for walking. A look at it on the map will show that on the right it skirts along below the heights of Foilanumera and Mweelin and on the left for most of its course it overlooks the headwaters of many tributaries of the Sullane river and offers many fine views of the Paps, Knocknabro and even of the Boggeraghs. For most of its length it is a 'cliff' road which clings on to steep slopes. For future reference it will be referred to as the Foilanumera road.

For the first 0.5 mile or so you pass through a certain amount of forestry and then into more open country as the road takes a major loop to the right in order to maintain its height. As you fall slightly towards the head of the loop you appear to be heading straight into a massive wall of rock but of course the road turns left before you 'hit' it. At the top of the loop a road from Coolea comes in on the left and just beyond the junction you get a particularly good view of the highlights of the Derrynasaggarts. You now pass through some forestry and slowly the road rises up to a shallow col between Mweelin (1,605 ft) on the right and an unnamed peak (1,408 ft) on the left. As you arrive at the highest point of the rise you will notice on your right an unsurfaced road climbing up the side of Mweelin. This is a component of the next walk.

And now, having come through the col the view changes completely as the Shehy mountains and the Lee valley take over the vista and, as you continue, the whole of the Bunsheelin basin opens up once more hemmed in by Lackabaun, the heights above Gougane Barra and the Pass of Keimaneigh. Finally the road curves around the rim of the basin and arrives at the Mouth of the Glen where you turn right and walk the last 0.5 mile downhill to your car with that glorious view ahead.

Distance: almost 15 miles. Time: about 6 hours.

14
Mweelin Mountain

Reference has been made in the previous walk (p. 81) to Mweelin mountain (G.R. 130 716) and to the unsurfaced road (not on the map) that goes up the side of it from the Foilanumera road at G.R. 140 714. You will come down this road towards the end of this walk. Mweelin rises above the Bunsheelin basin and forms the north-east side of the rim thereby affording the lower regions perfect shelter from the cold north and east winds of winter. The highest point (1,605 ft) is easily accessible and offers a complete 360 degree panoramic view of Cork and Kerry.

The walk to be decribed is a superb one which offers the very best of Bunsheelin scenery and of the upper Lee valley and its surrounds. It has about 5 miles in common with the Lackabaun walk and thereby is an attractive alternative for anyone who may find the Lackabaun walk too long. A word of advice however: do not attempt it immediately after a period of heavy rain. Select a day which follows at least three or four dry days.

Leave your car at the same spot as for the Lackabaun walk and follow that walk for the first 3.5 miles as far as the road which branches off to the right near the shed surrounded by farm machinery. This road has already been referred to (p. 79). It is marked on the map and it climbs high up among the slopes of the Bunsheelin basin. The G.R. of the junction is 126 698. Take this road and follow it up through the trees as it rises fairly steeply and passes a number of homesteads. After about a mile it comes out into open country at which stage it has lost its tarmacadam and abruptly changes to a rough narrow track which can be seen ahead as it zig-zags up to greater heights. At this point below on your left is a large shed belonging to the local sheep farmer. On your right there is a fenced green field and you can dodge the first stretch of the track (which has virtually been obliterated through the construction of the fence) by cutting across the field upward to the far corner where there is a gate and where you meet the track just where it begins to rise quite steeply as it swings north. The upward slog is compensated for by the superb views of the Inchigeelagh lakes and their surronding heights and of the green Bunsheelin basin and its heights with the Kerry peaks peeping through here and there. At the point where the track (now more akin to the dried up bed of a mountain stream) levels out, it suddenly becomes once more a road, albeit an unsurfaced one and this shortly arrives at a T junction where you turn right.

The unsurfaced road on to which you turn is the road (already referred to) which comes up to the other side of Mweelin from the Foilanumera road. It is a 'turf road' which is still used by the locals who draw turf from the extensive bogland up here. In summer time – especially on Saturdays – you are likely to meet many turf cutters. Very often entire families come up to help with the work bringing along their picnic meals which they cook on the spot on turf fires. Enjoy the unique aromatic blend of turf smoke and cooking food!!

Having come up the side of the Bunsheelin basin at a slant – in contrast to the Lackabaun track which goes straight up – and made your right-hand turn on to the level 'turf road' you will see ahead of you on the left up on a height a concrete marker. This marks the top of Mweelin. Scramble up to it for that great 360 degree view already referred to. The whole of West Cork and the best of Kerry is there before you.

Return to the road turning left on to it of course and follow it the whole way down to the Foilanumera road with magnificent views of the Lee Valley and the Shehys. Turn right at the junction and back to your car as in Walk 13.

Distance: 8 miles. Time: about 3 hours.

15
The Coom Wood Circuit

Having read the accounts of the Lackabaun and Mweelin walks and if they appear to be somewhat daunting why not try instead a very enjoyable walk of about 5 miles. It will give you some of the flavour of this region of the Derryna-saggarts.

It starts at Ballyfinnane Bridge (G.R: 140 744) which is approached via Coolea from Ballyvourney by turning left in the village at the signpost to Coolea. For most of its course to Coolea and beyond the road keeps close to the Sullane river. It is a pleasant road.

Coolea village is interesting inasmuch as it has a church, a school and a post-office but it has no drinking establishment with the result that its inhabitants have either to go down to Ballyvourney or up to Coom – to the Highest Pub in Ireland!! Beyond Coolea the road continues to rise, affording some good long-distance views to the right of the County Bounds and ahead of Foilanumera. Shortly after you come out into open country you will see Ballyfinnane bridge ahead of you. There is adequate parking space here and you now start walking on the road to the right just before the bridge.

For over 2 miles the road climbs up through old trees to the Cork–Kerry border at Coom. You are really walking up to Coom wood or what is left of it. Soon up on your left you will see the line of the Foilanumera road (described in Walk 13) which is your way forward from the top. Having reached the top of Coom turn sharp left at the junction onto the Foil-anumera road, the course of which has been described in Walk 13.

Your walk continues along the this road to the top of the big loop already referred to in Walk 13 but long before you get to the top of the loop you will see a road coming up to meet you away to your left and when you arrive at the junction turn left and begin the descent back to Ballyfinnane Bridge. The immediate surroundings are barren but the distant views of the Derrynasaggart high spots are very fine.

Distance: 5 miles. Time: about 2 hours.

The Shehy Mountains

Sheet 24 indicates the Shehy Mountains as the area immediately south and east of Gougane Barra lake (G.R: W 090 664)
and including the four prominent landmarks cited in some
of the previous walks, namely Doughill (1,553 ft), Douce
(1,564 ft), Shehy mountain itself (not named on map but
height given as 1,795 ft) and Nowen Hill (1,763 ft). Unlike
the Boggeragh and Derrynasaggart areas it is not easy to as-
sign natural boundaries for the area so we shall let the col-
lection of walks determine the area's extent. In this way we
arrive at an area bounded on the east by a line from Inchigeelagh (G.R: W 222 662) to Dunmanway (G.R: W 230 530),
on the south by the Dunmanway–Bantry road (R586), on the
west by the Bantry–Glengarriff–Kenmare road (N71) and on
the north by the top edge of the map as far as Inchigeelagh.
A small part of Walk 16 lies beyond this edge.

Of the three walking areas the Shehy area is without
doubt, the most delightful. For sheer beauty it outstrips the
Derrynasaggarts and the Boggeraghs. The peaks are somewhat lower (only one, Knockboy, over 2,000 ft) and the area
considerably 'greener'. The lowlands are also more fertile
and then the lighting seems to be different and it seems to
emphasise the vast variety of flora. It is quite possible that
the greater proximity of the area to the sea and the way it is
sheltered from the cold north is responsible for these amel-
iorating effects. Finally the area has an extensive network of
deserted byroads which wind and climb and fall thus offering a frequent change of scene often every few hundred
yards. In fact it is a walker's paradise. ·

All the walks described except Number 16 are south and
west of the Lee river and a number of them are set in the
mountainous area between the Lee and the Bandon river to
the south. Furthermore they are all (apart from part of Walk
16) on Sheet 24. However, in regard to grid references they
straddle two Sub-Zones, V and W. Hence grid references in
this section include the appropriate Sub-Zone letter.

16

Viewing Gougane Barra on foot – and much more as well

Gougane Barra with its lake, its oratory and its forest walks all set amidst wild surroundings has become extremely popular with tourists from far and near. The idyllic lake set in a long deep valley closed on all sides except the east, the trees, the rocks, the deep green pasture, the striking cascades, a little hiberno-romanesque architecture all combine to give the source of the river Lee an unsurpassed, wild and lonely beauty.

Most of the many visitors arrive at the lake via the road which runs up from the Inchigeelagh–Bantry road (R584) that goes through the nearby striking Pass of Keimaneigh. This places them on the same level as the lake and even if they decide to walk/drive up through the magnificent forest park the trees obscure the lake. Now this walk will enable you to see Gougane Barra from a number of vantage points high above the lake as well as from the level of the lake itself without ever leaving road.

Since the walk lies partly on Sheet 21 and partly on Sheet 24 it is suggested that you get the route clear by studying it carefully on the two sheets before you set out at all. So for a start line up the two sheets using the red grid reference numbers in the margins to do so: then let the margin of one sheet overlap that of the other. The starting point is on Sheet 21. It is a road junction of G.R: W 145 685 immediately below the name 'Carrig Lo' on the map. At the time of writing there is a signpost here to Macroom on the one hand and Ballingeary–Gougane Barra on the other. The 'branch' road has no sign and this is the one to take in spite of the directive of the signpost to Gougane Barra. You will recognise it by the fact that immediately after the junction it crosses a stream and there is a home on the left above. This road is the

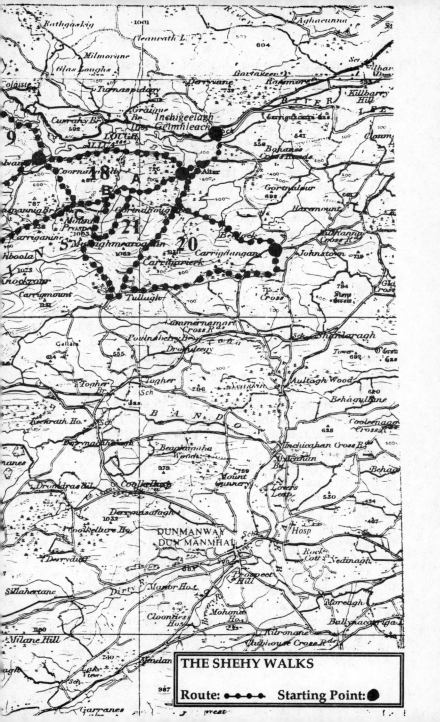

THE SHEHY WALKS

Route: •••• Starting Point: ●

one which runs along the length of the Bunsheelin river to the foot of Lackabaun and part of which you have walked if you have done Walk 13 or 14. Having followed this road for about a mile you turn left onto a narrower road signposted (at the time of writing) to Gougane Barra. This road makes a semicircle around the 964 ft-high hill and then (avoiding the turn to the left) strikes off (now on Sheet 24) to Gougane Barra where it strikes the lake at its eastern end. The road skirts the lake for a short distance and then swings away from it and finally joins R584 (referred to above) where a left turn and a signpost to Ballingeary direct you eastward for about 0.5 mile to the Keimaneigh Post Office just before which you take the turn to the left on the road which climbs up out of the valley and after about 2 miles, swings roughly eastward (back on Sheet 21) to the starting point. The route is thus a rough figure of 8, the crossover being the short stretch of link road (Sheet 21) connecting the outward journey with the return one but on which you do not walk. If, as a result of reading this rather lengthy preamble, you feel that the whole thing is too complicated, do not abandon such a fine walk. The signposts will help you at most of the critical points.

On summer days and on fine Sunday afternoons throughout the year there can be heavy tourist traffic on the road from the lake down to the R584 and on the R584 itself so select your day and time carefully. A fine crisp sunny winter's day can be most impressive. Even if the colours are somewhat dimmed the many streams and cascades are in spate and some of these are quite spectacular. Try to get to the starting point about 10.30 am. The sun will then be behind you for the first half of the walk lighting up what is in front of you. If done in the reverse direction the walk is somewhat less splendid as the good views are behind you.

The starting point may be approached by two different ways from Macroom. The first is via the Mouth of the Glen as described in Walk 13 but instead of parking near the top of the pass you follow the road down towards Ballingeary for just over a mile until you come to the junction described above. The second way is to drive east out of Macroom on the N22 for about 0.25 mile to its junction with the R584 signposted to Gougane Barra and Glengarriff where you turn right (or left if you are coming from Cork). This is the lovely road that runs along by the Geragh (see Walk 9), crosses the Toon river by Toon Bridge and on to Inchigeel-agh and then winds its way along the north shore of Lough Allua to Ballingeary where at the eastern end of the village you turn right on a road which rises for about a mile to the starting point. Both ways are equally beautiful and it is re-commended that you go one way and return by the other.

Parking close to the starting point is a little difficult. Some little distance back up towards the Mouth of the Glen close to the ditch will provide safety. An alternative is on the road up from Ballingeary just about 100 yards below the starting point near a house on the left (if you are coming from Ballingeary) where there is a grass margin also on the left. This point is about half-way between the starting point and the finishing point.

Head off over the cascading stream as it falls sharply soon to join the Bunsheelin on its way down to Ballingeary. You will get glimpses of it here and there as you walk along this delightful undulating road. Notice the heights of Mwee-lin (Walk 14) ahead to your right and the cliffs of Lackabaun straight ahead. Notice also the rich green pasture on your left – alluvial soil washed down from the heights. After about a mile you come to your turn left crossing the Bun-sheelin itself and then rising rapidly between trees up to the rim of the Bunsheelin basin. As you rise enjoy the good views ahead and behind on the right. When you get to the rim the road falls slightly passing what appears to be a de-serted farmstead and soon you come to a road coming in on the left. This is the link referred to in the figure of 8 above. Pass this by and likewise a road going to the right shortly afterwards. This latter is a cul-de-sac. You are now in a high plain on a road which is level for over a mile. Soon, off on your left Doughill appears and the heights behind Gougane Barra hove into sight ahead and a little later Shehy and Douce appear and then you get a very fine view of the deep cutting which is the Pass of Keimaneigh lying between

Doughill on the west and Foilastookeen (1698 ft) on the east.

The road now rises slightly to a cluster of trees surrounding a derelict homestead and then quite suddenly the whole vista of Gougane Barra lies below you and as you descend; the lake, the island with its oratory, the towering heights, the forestry and the cascades all unfold. Enjoy the view as you continue to descend – now more steeply – to lake-level, noticing as you go the strikingly green pasture and the little slab footbridge leading to a homestead. Down at lake-level the road swings left (south). Two bridges close together cross the infant Lee as it leaves the lake. Continue to the T junction where you turn left to continue the walk. The right-hand turn will take you along the edge of the lake to the oratory and onward to the forestry where there is a very fine circular walk but it is on the road and there may be much traffic.

Back now on the trail from the lake down to the R584. This is about a mile of delightful falling, winding road. Initially there is forestry on your right and on your left you can hear the Lee as it falls through rocky channels and gorse. After about 0.5 mile you get a good view of the heights of Doughill ahead and you finally arrive at the junction with R584 where you turn left towards Ballingeary. The best advice for your 0.5 mile on this road is set a brisk pace turning left on to the narrow road immediately before the Post Office.

This road crosses a stream first and then slightly further on the Lee, now much wider, and then it begins to rise quite steeply for over 0.5 mile. There is plenty of gaps in the trees to enable you to view the Pass and its surrounding heights. By now the road has acquired a healthy green spine and you have passed two homesteads. Just where the road comes into open country and levels out a look back to the left will give you yet a different view of Gougane Barra away below.

As you continue eastward you are parallel with the road you took into Gougane Barra and you can see it across the moor on your left. This is a grand stretch of open road with good views in all directions. It now falls through forestry for about 0.5 mile until you come to a junction to the left which you do not take (this is the other end of the link already referred to). Back now on Sheet 21 your road continues level but now amid softer surroundings with good views of the Lee valley and beyond on your right. About 1.25 mile from the junction it falls fairly steeply down to the Bunsheelin river which it crosses and rises again to join the Ballingeary road a very short distance below the starting point.

Distance: 8 miles. Time: about 3.5 hours (both exclusive of any walking or time spent at Gougane Barra).

17

The Old Road from Inchigeelagh to Bantry Bay or the Gortloughra Road

As an introduction to this great 14 mile walk it is worthwhile to look at Bantry Bay on Sheet 24 – that deep broad, 35 mile long inlet of the Atlantic Ocean and to notice the large number of roads that descend to its headwaters from the surrounding country. Some of them stretch for many miles inland and between them they connect virtually every in-land town and village in West Cork with the sea. A number of them have been there for over a thousand years and have seen the movement of millions of people. Some of these old roads have adapted themselves to become part of the present-day national and regional network while others have declined in importance and have become minor roads – even tracks in some cases. This walk takes you on one of these old declined routes from the Lee valley at Inchigeelagh towards Bantry Bay.

It is easy to identify it on the map where it is depicted as a minor road. Starting from Inchigeelagh village it crosses the Lee and swings south-west almost in a straight line between Shehy and Douce mountains to Kealkil village (G.R: W 046 556) which is about 3.5 miles from Bantry Bay. Three roads from the hinterland converge on Kealkil – the afore-mentioned, the R584 which has come also from Inchigeelagh through the Keimaneigh Pass and the R585 which has come via the Cousane Gap (G.R: W 132 570). United they follow the Owvane River down to Bantry Bay.

The actual walk is from Inchigeelagh to Kealkil. It is a long, quiet walk full of contrasting landscapes and views and it requires very little directional assistance to follow it. Unfortunately it is not a circular walk (a solution for the re-turn to Inchigeelagh is offered at the end). Nevertheless walks to be subsequently described (18, 21 and 22) embody sections of it and these are circular walks. The road is known locally as the Gortloughra Road. This is the name which will be used in reference to it in subsequent walks. Gortloughra is one of the major townlands through which it passes.

Having come from Macroom or Cork via the N22 and the R584 you will find ample parking in Inchigeelagh village. A word of warning before setting off: it is a long walk and there is no shop or hostelry whatsoever along the way.

Turn south at Creedon's Hotel over the Lee to a T junction at which you turn right, signposted South Lake Road. This South Lake Road runs westward along the south shore of Lough Allua to the western end of Ballingeary village. It is superb for scenery and will be described fully in walks 18 and 19. On this walk you tread about the first 1.25 mile of it with good views here and there ahead to Douce and Lackabaun. Within the first 0.5 mile from the T junction you will pass two roads going left in quick succession. Shortly afterwards you will pass a signposted Mass Rock on your left and at 1.5 mile you will come to a fork where the South Lake Road forms the right-hand prong and falls. You take the left-hand prong which rises and this is the beginning of the Gortloughra road.

It has been mentioned that sections of the Gortloughra road form parts of subsequent walks. To facilitate the easy identification of these sections, certain road junctions along its course will be labelled with a capital letter – A, B, C, etc. Furthermore, distances quoted are taken from Inchigeelagh and not from the starting point of the road.

The first 0.75 mile is a gradual ascent through shrubs and forestry (the surfaced road to the left is a cul-de-sac) after which you come into more open country with a view of Shehy ahead. The road now falls gently through a cluster of homes, known as Meall (not marked) and continues falling as it passes a road taking off to the left (point A). Having bridged a small stream flowing towards the Lee your road now rises steeply but soon the gradient becomes much easier. This is pleasant walking although forestry restricts the range of view somewhat.

At about 3.25 miles the road levels out and there is a road branching to the left (point B) which climbs up to Mount Prospect (Walk 21). Shortly there is a road to the right (point C) which descends to the South Lake Road. Off to your right there is a distant view of Mullaghanish and the western peaks of the Derrynasaggarts. Forestry takes over again and you pass a rustic sign in Irish pointing to a children's burial place where infants who died prior to baptism were buried. The road rises and passes what was Toureen-alour school, now a private home. Notice the fine stonework of house and surrounding wall. A bridge labelled Drohida-spaunig carries the road over a stream flowing south from Shehy to the Lee and after a further gentle climb the forestry gives way to open country with views to the right of the Derrynasaggarts and ahead of Douce and craggy Doughill.

The climb up over the shoulder of Shehy now commences. At 5.25 miles a road to the right falls into the valley and then rises and can be seen going away up the side of Douce and over Doughill. It then continues north and ultimately joins the R584 some miles west of Ballingeary. One might think that this would make a good walk. It is rather disappointing as much of it is through forestry and some farmstead high up on Doughill seems to specialise in breeding bulls!!

Soon the 900 ft contour is crossed and after a few undulations the road reaches its highest point at about 7 miles and you are in direct line with the top of Douce on the right and there is a complete change of scene. And what a magnificent scene. First, look at that grand beckoning stretch of road ahead of you – almost 2 miles of it. It gradually falls away down the slopes of Shehy to a broad marsh area at the foot of Douce and then rises and disappears away over a distant crest. Further away beyond Douce are the heights bordering the R584 as it falls towards Kealkil and beyond lie the great heights on the far side of the Coomhola River including Coomhola Mountain (1561 ft) itself. Straight ahead is the hinterland of Bantry Bay and, if the day is right, at this point you get your first glimpse of Bantry Bay itself.

Enjoy the long descent to Gortloughra bridge close to

which there is a road to the right (point D) which skirts the southern slopes of Douce (Walk 22). Now follow the gradual rise up from the bridge through open country to the crest where the view west is superb. It is worth the extra effort to climb the gate on the right and follow the track a short distance to its highest point just to get the best of the view.

Away to the far west are the Caha Mountains – the spine of the Beara peninsula including the cone-shaped Sugarloaf (1,887 ft) behind Glengarriff and far beyond the flat top of Hungry Hill (2,251 ft) behind Adrigole and of course, nearer to you are the waters of Bantry Bay. This is West Cork at its best and great walking. You are now well over half way at 9.5 miles. As you coast down the gentle slope you get an even better view of Bantry Bay itself – straight out to the ocean.

With the gradual descent, trees and shrubs begin to appear along the sides of the road, The junction to the right (point E) takes one over to the R584 (Walk 22). At about 11.5 miles the best of the walk is over as the road has fallen and levelled out along the Owvane valley and trees obscure the long-distance views. Nevertheless it is most pleasant and peaceful walking. Soon the Owngar River coming down from Cousane Gap is crossed and at 13 miles you join the road from the Cousane Gap and having turned right continue into Kealkil.

Distance: almost 14 miles. Time: 5 hours.

In regard to returning to Inchigeelagh: to retrace one's steps is not practical; to get a friend to drive the car along the R584 to Kealkil is a luxury; you could walk north out of Kealkil village to the R584 and hitch a lift – not too difficult as traffic is frequent and West Corkonians are generous. However the best solution to the problem is the fact that there is a once-a-week bus service between Macroom and Bantry via Inchigeelagh and Kealkil and vice-versa on the R584. At the time of writing the day of the week is Saturday and the bus departs Kealkil at 4.20 pm for Inchigeelagh.

18

A Circle around Cooraghreenane and Coornahahilly

Cooraghreenane and Coornahahilly are two rounded wooded hills of height 726 ft and 817 ft – on the south shore of Lough Allua close to its eastern end. The G.R. of the mid-point between them is W 194 648. The former is not actually named on the map. Having identified them you will see that their bases are neatly circled by road and this in fact is your walk, the highlight of which is the 3 mile stretch along the shore of Lough Allua. It would be unfair to infer from this that the remainder of the walk is dull. On the contrary the other sections teem with good scenery and make excellent walking. The starting point is where the Gortloughra road and the South Lake road part (see Walk 17). Parking is difficult at this precise point but if you drive on for about 0.25 mile on the South Lake road you will come to a parking area associated with Cooraghreenane Wood on your left.

A word of advice at this point. The South Lake road is a tourist attraction. Therefore select a time other than Sunday and Saturday afternoon in the summer. In fact morning is the best time when – as you walk west – the sun is behind you and lighting up the magnificent views ahead.

For the first mile or so the road lies some distance from and above Lough Allua. It rises and falls, swings right and left now passing through woodland now through open country and all the time offering different views of the Lough with its islands and isthmuses and surrounding green slopes all against a backdrop of Mweelin, Lackabaun and the heights around Gougane Barra. Now and again you will cross a fast-flowing stream on its way from the heights on your left to Lough Allua.

After about 1.5 mile the road falls to the lake level and remains there for the next 1.5 mile when it swings left slightly away from the water and you meet your left turn. You will easily recognise this turn because just ahead on the lake road you will see a fairly large bridge which carries the road over a goodly-sized stream flowing down from Douce.

Having swung left onto the road which will take you south to the Gortloughra road you very soon come to a Y junction where you take the left-hand arm. The right-hand arm is a cul-de-sac. You now have a climb of about 400 ft in the space of a mile but it is quite a pleasant one. At the start the road is somewhat closed in by steep slopes on each side but it soon gives way to more open country and after about 0.5 mile you should begin to look back now and again at Lough Allua – now away below you – and at the heights beyond.

You meet the Gortloughra road at the point C (see Walk 17) where you turn left on a slight rise with forestry on your right. You now head eastward on what is the first 2.5 miles in Walk 17. However the views are quite different from those of the westward trip. The stretches of open country afford some very fine views on your right of Mullaghmear-ogafin and Carrigarierk – to be described in subsequent walks. Ultimately you descend through the trees to the union of the Gortloughra road and the South Lake road where you turn left and back to your car.

Distance: 7 miles. Time: 2.5 hours.

19

A Circle in the Townland of Kealvaugh

This walk is the logical sequel to the previous one inasmuch as one leg of it covers the western part of the South Lake road which was not traversed previously and if you feel that the previous walk on its own is not long enough to warrant the car journey you can easily combine it with this one and thereby adding another 5.5 miles.

The starting point of the walk is a short distance on the other side of the bridge on the South Lake road just after where you left that road and turned left (south) in Walk 18. Its G.R. is W 166 650 and the route is clear from the map. It leaves the South Lake road by a narrow road which first heads south-west and away from Lough Allua. Having climbed up to 800 ft it turns north and descends to the South Lake road at a point about 2 miles west of the starting point. The walk roughly circles the townland of Kealvaugh which is marked on the map and it will be taken here, as outlined above, in a clockwise direction with the result that you will be walking eastward on the South Lake road. There is reasonable parking in the vicinity of the bridge.

The narrow road on which you take off from the South Lake road is a pleasant one which soon develops a green spine and for the first mile or so you have the company on the left of a fast-flowing stream coming down from Shehy and Douce to Lough Allua. Avoid the unsurfaced roads to the left and continue the climb into open country where one sees Shehy and Douce ahead together with the Gortloughra countryside.

The highest point is reached in about 2 miles and the climb has been fairly stiff but the view is worth it. Down below is Ballingeary village and the Lee. Rising above them is the rim of the Bunsheelin basin near the Mouth of the Glen while away in the distance to the east is Mullaghanish and Musheramore and even the tip of Cooper's Rock (Walk 3). Looking westward one sees the heights of the north-western side of the Shehys – Conigar (1,889 ft) and Foilastooken (1,698 ft) away beyond the Keimaneigh Pass.

Whatever about the steepness of the upward trek, that of the descent is even greater; the same 800 ft but this time in about 1 mile. The superb views on the heights gradually give way to nearby green pastures and trees and you ultimately join the South Lake road where you turn right.

Along here the road is narrow and enclosed by trees but not dense enough to prevent you from enjoying pleasant glimpses of the Lee on the left. At 1.5 mile from the junction the road moves away from the fertile fields and rises into an open countryside of gorse and stones with very fine views eastward. It soon begins to descend to the bridge where you left your car.

Distance: 5.5 miles. Time: 2 hours.

20
The Carrigarierk Circle

Carrigarierk is a large dome-shaped hump (1130 ft) lying about 4 miles south of Inchigeelagh and marked on the map. Its G.R. is W 210 622. In English its name would be Rock of the View and it certainly lives up to its name. Much of it has been re-afforested. This walk takes you around its periphery.

Immediately to the west of Carrigarierk and separated from it by a road running north-east – south-west is an equally craggy hump (1062 ft) also marked on the map – Mullaghmearogafin which translates to Top of Finn's Forefinger!! Walk 21 traverses its periphery. Thus, Walks 20 and 21 have that road referred to above in common. It rises to a height of over 900 ft and passes between the two humps by a short gap. It is probably the finest stretch of road for scenery in West Cork.

The original 1-inch Ordnance Survey Map of the area carries a name on this road: Knockaunnabipee – a frightful phonetic massacre of the Irish *Cnocan na bPiobai* which translates to Hillock of the Pipes. Hillock is something of an understatement as you will discover when you walk it!! It is now and has been for some time known locally as Pipe Hill. In regard to the origin of the name, the following story was gleaned some years ago from an elderly resident of the area. The parish of Uibh Laoghaire of which Inchigeelagh is the centre (not geographical) stretches south across the Lee almost as far as the Bandon River. When parishioners in that side of the parish died their coffined bodies were borne on shoulders north on Pipe Hill to the church in Inchigeelagh. When the funeral procession reached the top, it rested while the bearers lit their pipes and had a smoke before starting the long descent – the tobacco being provided by the relatives of the deceased. As you climb up the southern side of Pipe Hill you might think of what it would have been like if you were one of the six under a heavy coffin!!

But to get on to the walk. It is roughly a quadrilateral and it can be commenced at any one of the four corners. In order to make the best of its scenic potential and to make it complementary to Walk 21 the north-east corner will be the starting point here. This is a crossroad of G.R: W 242 624 on the Inchigeelagh–Dunmanway road about 3 miles from the former. To get there from Inchigeelagh turn south over the Lee and bear left at the T junction shortly after the bridge keeping straight at Bohane's Cross Roads, skirting around the heights of Gortalour on your left and passing the little Killhanna Lough on your right. The relevant crossroad is easily recognised by the steeply falling road coming in on your left with Killhanna school clearly visible a few yards up this road which is signposted to Johnstown. There is plenty of safe parking on the grass margin near the cross.

A close look at the map indicates what is very like a cross of 5 roads rather than 4 with 2 minor roads taking off on the western side, one roughly going south-west and the other north-west. The former has more or less disappeared. You take the latter which offers 2.25 miles of delightful walking with a green spine all the way. It rises, falls, winds and crosses many fast-flowing streams on their way from Carrigarierk to Lough Allua. Gorse, wild flowers, sloes, blackberries, red-berried holly – each in its own season – grow in profusion along its hedgerows. The few homesteads are sheltered by clusters of old trees while further afield rocks stand out of green pasture. Here and there at the occasional gateway on the right you will catch glimpses of the distant Paps and Mullaghanish. As you make the final mild descent to the junction with Pipe Hill you see ahead of you on the right the western end of Lough Allua. You turn left at the junction.

You join Pipe Hill over a mile from its northern end just where the gradient begins to stiffen. In fact just below you is a hairpin bend. There is a grotto nearby. As you begin the long haul to the top you soon come into open barren country. After about 0.5 mile just where the top of Shehy appears over the high ground ahead notice, just in off the road, on your right a good example of a Lios – a circular fortification in the form of an earthen ditch. As you go higher do not forget to have the occasional look back across that great landscape to the north. Most importantly do not forget to look back before you walk through the gap at the top.

Off in the distance to the north-west are the Kerry mountains with the heights around Keimaneigh to the front. As your eye moves towards the north you see the well-known peaks of the Derrynasaggarts and finally, in the east, Musheramore crowning the Boggeraghs. Below you is the Gortloughra road as it winds westwards through Meall and beyond; set in a hilly frame is Lough Allua. For the full grand view make your way across the bracken to the actual top of Carrigarierk. It takes only about 10 minutes to get there and there are the remains of an old 'turf road' which takes off from precisely the top of Pipe Hill.

Standing in the gap you are on the watershed between the Lee to the north and the Bandon river to the south and, as you make the steep descent, you are looking across the sloping (to the east) plain carved out by the Bandon and its tributaries all of which rise on Shehy or Nowen. Incidentally notice how close you are to Shehy – just over there on your right. Beyond is Nowen. Soon the occasional tree appears nearby as you descend to lower levels and more fertile land. Incidentally there is plenty of red-berried holly around here but in October!!

At the foot of Pipe Hill in the townland of Tullagh take the first turn left on a rising road. Pass the turn on your right and swing left at the ensuing fork, rising all the while. The road climbs gently between rocky outcrops and, as you go, look back from time to time and enjoy the fine views of the heights between Shehy and Nowen and of the great bowl of fertile fields below them. On your left the craggy, partly wooded southern slopes of Carrigarierk keep you company as you travel east. Having passed the road going off on your right you enter a belt of forestry and soon after emerging from it you join the Inchigeelagh–Dunmanway road.

While you are at the junction (where you turn left) take careful note of its surroundings just in case you decide to reverse the direction of the walk on some future occasion.

Coming in the opposite direction on the Inchigeelag–Dunmanway road there is a number of right turns around here and it is important to take the correct one. And another word of advice: You will see from the map that your road back takes a big loop to the east before turning north in order to avoid the heights of Carrigdangan. You will also notice the very minor road on the map which forms the third side of the triangle. Do not be tempted to try it as a short cut. It is no longer a through road.

The mile-long walk back to the car is through pleasant farmland and there is a gentle ascent all the way. You may meet some traffic.

Distance: 9 miles. Time: 3 hours.

21
The Mullaghmearogafin Circle

No introduction to this walk is necessary provided you have read the previous walk. The route taken (counter-clockwise) is such that Pipe Hill is traversed south to north in contrast to the Carrigarierk walk.

The ideal starting point is the northern end of Pipe Hill at its junction with the South Lake road. The G.R. of this point is W 220 652. Parking is a bit difficult just here and it may be as well to drive on to the Cooraghreenane Wood parking area (where you parked for Walk 18) and retrace your steps to the first turn right which of course is the start of the Gortloughra road and you take to it.

You tread the first mile or so of the Gortloughra road (described in Walk 17) through Meall down the hill to point A which is the junction with a road going off to the left. Its G.R. is W 198 640. Having turned left onto it you follow its gentle fall to bridge a stream, then across a flat marsh area after which you begin to climb gently and wind. Avoid the unsurfaced road going to the left and continue uphill. After about a mile the road swings west and out into the more open country with some very fine views to the north of the Lee valley, the Derrynasaggarts and beyond. Immediately below, you see the little island in Lough Allua on which are the remains of a crannog. The road is now in barren country and it finally levels out at 814 ft as you approach a T junction where you turn left.

This road comes up from point B of the Gortloughra road and you are joining it at its highest point in a gap between Mulllaghmearogafin on the east and Mount Prospect (1,003 ft) on the west. As you journey down the steep winding descent you are looking at Shehy mountain just ahead of you and the upper basin of the Bandon river and its early tributaries. One of these is the Caha which you will soon cross. It is a fast-flowing stream tumbling through a narrow gorge from its source, Lough Nambrackderg, (Lake of the Red Trout) high on the slopes of Shehy. It joins the Bandon a few miles north of Dunmanway. Your road, which has now levelled out follows its course for the next 1.25 mile. Across the widening valley on your left are the southern slopes of Mullaghmearogafin. Having crossed the Caha again you immediately come to a junction with a road running roughly north-east–south-west where you turn left.

If by chance, you are interested in climbing Shehy now or on another outing this is the spot from which to start. Instead of turning left turn right and within less than 0.25 mile take the very minor road (suitable for a car if you wish to drive up there) going right. Along this road on your right the slopes of Shehy come down to meet you and you can take off whenever you feel like it. You are only about 1.5 mile and 1,100 ft from the top and one hour at the most will get you there and the going is never too difficult. The 360 degree view from the top is nothing short of magnificent. It is said that on a clear day Cork city can be seen from up there.

To return to the walk proper: you walk on this very pleasant road keeping left at the fork about 0.25 mile ahead and avoiding the right hand turn slightly further on. And now begins the steep climb up the southern side of Pipe Hill – 500 ft in just over a mile. Take your time to it and when you want a breather just stop and look back at the superb view already described in the previous walk. And, of course as you go through the gap at the top the whole vista changes suddenly. What was behind you in the last walk is now ahead of you and you can fully enjoy it as you coast down passing the junction on the right above the grotto. The gradient now eases as the road moves through pleasant green fields and lush foliage. Within 2.5 miles from the top you meet the South Lake road where you turn left and walk the very pleasant 0.5 mile to your car.

Distance: 8 miles. Time: about 3 hours.

You can lengthen this walk by a very pleasant 1.25 mile by

continuing on the Gortloughra road past point A to point B where you turn left on the road which at first rises gradually with forestry on the right. A short steep climb will bring you up to the Mullaghmearogafin–Mount Prospect gap.

It should be obvious now that many combinations of Walks 18, 20 and 21 are possible. Bear in mind that the direction of each can be reversed with little loss of scenic value. Between the 3 of them there are days and days of great walking.

22

Around the Townlands of Gortloughra and Cahermuckee

This is a short (about 6.5 miles) relatively easy pleasant walk with some fine views of Bantry Bay as seen from the southern slopes of Douce mountain. It is the ideal walk for the summer evening when the lowering sun casts a beautiful soft light over the entire terrain. For anyone holidaying in Ballingeary or Inchigeelagh or even Macroom the drive is not too long. It is perhaps a bit too far to come from Cork just for it alone but then it could be combined with one of the other shorter Shehy walks to make a good day's outing.

The starting point is at St Macomog's school on the Keimaneigh road, R584 just over 2 miles down from the Pass on the Bantry side. Its G.R. is W 096 598. Having located this point on the map it is easy to trace the route: along the very minor road which skirts the southern side of Douce to Gortloughra bridge (point D of Walk 17), south-west on the Gortloughra road to the turn right at point E and north to join the R584 less than a mile below the starting point.

There is ample parking close to the signpost in front of the school. The walk commences on the minor road which slopes down past the school to the Owvane river which has its source up near the Pass between Doughill and Douce. You are now walking on the stretch of road from the Pass to the school which preceded the present road. This earlier road kept close to the Owvane but at its northern end took a very sharp steep climb up to the Pass. It was of course, to avoid this steep pull that the present road was constructed along the shoulder of the valley.

Notice the fine view of Douce ahead of you and of Shehy slightly to the right. Avoid the right-hand turn shortly beyond the school and, after about 0.5 mile, go right at the junction. At this point you leave the old Pass road which

109

continues along by the river and you now cross the river and begin the climb away from its little valley and, as you get to the top of the steep S bend, you get your first glimpse of Bantry Bay and Sheep's Head (Muntervary) – the headland on its southern side. As you top the highest point Shehy is ahead of you while nearer at hand you see the Gortloughra road winding uphill away to the east. You are now well up on the slopes of Douce which towers above you on the left with Doughill and the Pass more or less behind you. The winding fall down to the Gortloughra road is gentle and full of ever-changing landscapes.

The bridge near which you turn right derives its name from the townland of Gortloughra. You now follow the gradually rising road ahead to point E (as already described in Walk 17). This is the best stretch (about 2.5 miles) of the Gortloughra road for views of Bantry Bay and it surrounding peninsulas.

It is not difficult to identify your turn right (point E) in the townland of Cahermuckee where you begin the short descent to the Owvane river which you re-cross before joining the R584.

You may well encounter considerable traffic on the R584 but you will be back at your car well within 20 minutes.

Distance: 6.5 miles. Time: 2.5 hours.

This walk is equally fine when done in the reverse direction namely walking from your car down the R584 to the left turn at Cahermuckee. It has the advantage that the stretch on the R584 is downhill and hence you will have to tolerate traffic for a shorter spell. The disadvantage is that the good views on the Gortloughra road are behind you.

23
The High Terrain between the Owvane and Coomhola Rivers

A look at the map shows that the Owvane and Coomhola rivers enter Bantry Bay within about a mile of each other having pursued converging courses from their respective sources. The high ground between them is topped by Conigar (1,886 ft). This walk explores some of the lower stretches of this high ground – a countryside which is little known. The walk does not match up to the scenic splendour of some of the other walks in the Shehy area. Nevertheless it offers views from a new angle of some of the landmarks of the area.

The starting point is – like that of Walk 22 – on the Bantry side of Keimaneigh on the R584 about 2.5 miles beyond St Macamog's school. It is a road turning off to the right with a signpost to a cottage industry making candles some distance up the road. The G.R. of the junction is W 066 578. The circle walk comprises following the R584 from this junction down to the outskirts of Kealkil village and leaving it for a rising, winding road up to Bull's Pocket and on to Lough Atooreen where you head north-west to the townland of Maugha whence you cross the Owenbeg river and turn south back to the R584.

It is better to do it in the clockwise direction described here as this will enable you to get the 0.75 mile stretch on the busy R584 over at the outset. For parking, the best thing to do is to turn right off the R584 into the road on which you will return and leave the car on the grassy margin.

The 0.75 mile on the gradually falling R584 is not very exciting since the road has now lost much of its height and hence its views. The right-hand road at the statue of St Finbarr is the one for you but just before you take it walk the few yards to the left and onto the bridge beneath which is the tumbling Owvane having just descended over a magnificent cataract – one of the best in West Cork.

Back on the byroad you pass Carriganass (Rock of the Waterfall) Castle which stands on the said rock. You soon leave the Owvane as the road swings northward across a plain at the far end of which you cross the Owenbeg river – a tributary of the Owvane and of which you will see more as the walk progresses.

Very shortly after crossing the Owenbeg there is a junction and it is important to take the left-hand arm since the right-hand one ends in a cul-de-sac about 2 miles up the Owenbeg valley as is clear from the map. Your road now begins to rise and as it does you get fine views behind you of Shehy and the fertile land between the Owvane and the Owngar. Soon Bantry Bay appears away to your left and as the road winds higher, you see different stretches of the bay now on your left and now behind you. The final pull up to Bull's Pocket is quite sharp and, as you near the top, look back at all the now familiar landmarks of Shehy country.

Bull's Pocket (origin of name unknown) is a short narrow pass and when you come out on the other side there is a completely new view, namely the great heights surrounding the Coomhola river – on the far side the peaks of Coomhola Mountain (1,561 ft) and Knockboy (2,321 ft) and on the near side Conigar (1,886 ft) while just below you sparkles Lough Atooreen. About 0.25 mile brings you down on level with the lake to a crossroad.

The road going on straight goes down to the Coomhola valley. The road on the left runs south-west towards the head of Bantry Bay while the road to the right (which is the one for you) goes up to Maugha. This is clearly at odds with the earlier printings of Sheet 24 which do not show these 4 roads meeting at a cross. Just as you turn the corner notice the very fine stone alignment on your right in the angle between the 2 roads. It is worth climbing over the gate and up into the field just to enjoy the majestic view from the site.

The road to Maugha is a fine open road for most of the way with mountain views off ahead and to the left. It was once surfaced but most of the surface has now disappeared –

especially in the upper reaches. The summer months see many turf cutters up here in the bogs on the right-hand side. In slightly over 1.5 mile from the stone alignment a grove ahead indicates a homestead where the good people will indicate to you the now disused stony track down by the side of the garden to the Owenbeg river, where a set of secure stepping stones will enable you to cross to the muddy track on the other side which climbs up from the bank and within a few yards reaches the surfaced road where you turn right.

At this point it is worthwhile to sit on the grassy bank and take in the scene. Across the Owenbeg to the north are Conigar with Foilastookeen to the right. Turning to the left off in the distance is Coomhola mountain and beyond it the many distant peaks of the Caha range in Beara. Near at hand the road falls down eastward to a junction, the left-hand arm of which crosses the Owenbeg by a bridge and climbs up the side of Conigar skirting the forestry. It ends at a farmstead. The right-hand arm is also a cul-de-sac up in the townland of Cappaboy Beg. There is a strange, wild, lonely beauty about this place especially on a sunny day. One cannot however help visualising the hard life of the many homes that once were up here where little is plentiful except water, fresh air and scenery.

Now to the road back which rises gently with Knockboy mountain off on the right and further beyond the Sugarloaf behind Glengarriff. After about 0.5 mile the road begins to fall and the foliage becomes more dense but not before you get glimpses of Bantry Bay. The candle house is passed on the right and as the road continues to fall there are good views of Douce and Shehy. After a pleasant 2 miles from where the Owenbeg was crossed you arrive back at the junction with the R584.

Distance: 7 miles. Time: 2.5 hours.

It may be worth pointing out here that while the Coomhola valley road may look attractive for walking from the map, it really is not until one gets up high on it near the Cork–Kerry border and then there is really no convenient circular walk.

113

24

Castle Donovan and Mullaghmesha

The irregular hump of Mullaghmesha (1629 ft, slightly lower than Shehy and Nowen but slightly higher than Douce and Doughill) may be regarded as the most southerly peak of the Shehy range. Its G.R. is W 090 516 and it lies just south-west of the Nowen Hill massif and is separated from it by a sort of valley whose floor falls and whose mouth opens towards the south. At the valley mouth there is a convergence of 5 roads and the scene is dominated by the ruined 16th century castle of the O'Donovan clan (Castle Donovan in Gothic script on the map) standing on a limestone outcrop at the eastern side close to where the 5 roads come together. One may regard this spot as the Castle Donovan to which the few signposts in the area direct one although there is no village, not even a hamlet. There are, however, quite a few houses along the valley floor, on its lower slopes and also in the more fertile land to the south of the valley mouth; hence the school which, apart from the castle, is the only other landmark.

The landscape around here is different from that of the more northerly Shehy area. It is difficult to describe that difference which manifests itself as soon as you come near the southern slopes of Nowen Hill. It seems to derive from the very sharp demarcation between the stony barren heights and the very rich green fields lower down. From the walker's point of view the difference shows itself in that the good views (and there are some great ones) are largely of the coastline (about 15 miles away) rather than of mountain and valley. Although there is a dense road network in the area suitable circular walks are scarce. Hence what is offered in the line of walking is itself different from the offerings in the other areas. Nevertheless it is hoped that you will find that the rather long trip from Macroom (24 miles) or Cork (44 miles) will have been worthwhile.

The suggested routes from Macroom and Cork are clearly marked in toto on the Ireland South Sheet. The best route to take from Macroom is the N22 east to its junction with R584 which you follow to Toon Bridge but instead of turning right for Inchigeelagh after the bridge you go straight on to the R587 which is well sign-posted all the way to Dunmanway via Glan Cross Roads and Shanalaragh (both marked on the map). At the eastern end of Dunmanway town you turn right onto the R586 and head for Drimoleague. In the middle of Drimoleague village you turn right passing the fairly new church on your left and head north, going straight at a crossroad about 1 mile on. After about another 2 miles you come to another cross (at which there is a co-op store) where you turn left and, within another mile you are at Castle Donovan. The entire route is quite a scenic one. The easiest route from Cork to Drimoleague is by the N71 to Bandon and from there, the R586 to Drimoleague via Dunmanway. The best parking at Castle Donovan is close to the school.

Just for the sake of becoming familiar with the scene it is suggested that, with Sheet 24 in hand, you walk the few yards westward from the school to the little bridge. Notice that the road on which you are is soon joined at a fork by another one from the east. Then there is the road going off on your right at the side of which is the castle. This is the one that runs north between Nowen and Mullaghmesha over to the Mealagh valley (more about this road later). Next there is the road to the left signposted to Bantry and immediately after that a very narrow one falling to the right. You will see from the map that this latter is a loop road and it forms part of the walk about to be described. You are now at the starting point of the walk on the road (shown on the map as 2 closely spaced lines) which rises steeply before you to the west.

This road is part of the very old walking one from the hinterland around Dunmanway to the coast at Bantry Bay. You can easily trace it in its entirety on the map as it runs almost in a straight line west from Dunmanway first along by the Dirty River, then between Nowen and Milane Hill to Leitry Bridge, to Castle Donovan, up over the south shoulder of Mullaghmesha and on to Bantry by Lough Bofinna. Whereas parts of it make good walking, much of it is dull and it does not measure up at all to, for example, the Gortloughra road (Walk 17) which is its counterpart about 6 miles to the north.

Incidentally from where you are standing or thereabouts you will notice a stony road going up high into Mullaghmesha. This is another one of these ubiquitous 'turf roads' (not on the map) which also forms part of the walk.

As you rise with the road you soon leave the soft green of the valley for more barren terrain. An unsurfaced road to the right after about 0.5 mile is a cul-de-sac. As the climb continues the view on the right and behind you gets better and better until the entire valley and away beyond it towards Dunmanway is in view. High ground on your left completely obscures any view to the south. About 1 mile from base the surfaced road to the right is the upper end of that loop already referred to. Very soon you come into open country; the road reaches its highest point (930 ft, Castle Donovan – 470 ft) and levels out and a great view to the south is before you.

This is the coastline of West Cork (on the average about 15 miles away) and, as you face it, to your left roughly is Rosscarbery Bay followed to the right by Glandore Harbour, Castletownsend, Toe Head and then you can see clearly the old tower on Spain Hill just behind Baltimore. Then come Sherkin Island and (more distant) the eastern end of the Clear Island. The view further west is obscured by Mount Kid in the middle distance but beyond, Mount Gabriel on the Mizen Peninsula hoves into view followed by the high points of the Dunmanus peninsula (Muntervary). Cast an eye too at the great expanse of green fields, forestry and homesteads that lies between you and the coastline. Continue on a few yards to where the road begins to fall for a very fine view of Bantry Bay as you look out over Whiddy Island towards flat-topped Hungry Hill and beyond as far as the eastern end of Bear Island. The Mizen Peninsula is again obscured – this time by nearby Bull Rock.

Ahead of you the road falls steeply and then the gradient becomes easier as it reaches more wooded and fertile terrain on its way down to Bantry town. Nowhere does one get a glimpse of Bantry town. It is tucked away in the eastern corner at the head of the bay and is obscured by the heights of Knocknaveagh which is immediately behind it.

Although pointers will be given later for incorporating the stretch of road which you have just trod into 2 circular walks it is suggested that now you retrace your steps to the junction with the upper end of the loop already referred to where you turn left. This is a grand walking road offering great views of Castle Donovan and the heights of Nowen. Soon, however, height is lost and the road begins to wind and passes through foliage by 2 homesteads fairly close together. A third homestead on your right has the back of its house to the road and directly opposite this an unsurfaced road rises off to the left. This is the 'turf road' already referred to and it is well worth walking its entire length of about 1.5 mile and back.

Shortly after you turn to the left you pass on your left a homestead painted white – outhouses and all and then you go through a gateway into open country with a little stream cascading down on your left. This is just one of very many which rise in the heights on both sides of the valley and flow southward to unite and become the Ilen River which flows by Skibbereen to Roaringwater Bay. As you continue to rise between the rocks and bracken you will see ahead of you on the right an enormous rock literally overhanging the road and, as you pass it, you wonder what is preventing it from crashing down on top of you. And there is an even bigger one up behind it! With every step you take the view to the left gets better and better.

Shortly after passing the 'hanging rock' the road swings northward and levels out somewhat but it soon begins its steep climb again and now you have that grand view of Bantry Bay out over those little blue lakes below you in the foreground. Tracks to the turf banks now begin to diverge on either side and finally the road itself peters out on a little plateau surrounded by turf banks at about 1,250 ft. Time now to stop and enjoy that great view of bay, headland, island, ocean, lake and mountain.

Just across from you is the ridge which is the highest point of Mullaghmesha. It is a pity that a track does not go as far as it for an even better view. If you do decide to head across the bogland to get to it be very careful; there is much very soft ground even in dry weather.

The return trip down is unbroken scenery all the way to the end where you turn left on the loop road which winds and falls down into the valley floor through fertile fields back to Castle Donovan.

Distance: 6 miles. Time: about 2.5 hours.

The Gowlane Road

Reference has already been make to the road that runs north past the castle to the Mealagh valley to the townland of Gowlane. It is well worth walking part – if not all – of this road. Having passed the castle on your left you continue along the eastern side of the valley floor but soon you begin to rise, gradually at first and then more steeply and the valley sides begin to close in and tower above you. After about 2 miles and a few hairpin bends you reach the highest point – a saddle at 1000 ft and then there is the very steep short drop via some more hairpin bends down to Gowlane with the views ahead of the Mealagh valley and the Maughanaclea Hills.

The walk back is perhaps better in that – having reached the saddle – you have the sea away in front of you and the lovely valley before you.

Distance (one way): 3 miles. Time: 1 hour.

A suggested short circular walk incorporating the Bantry old road.

Starting from Castle Donovan follow the Bantry old road west up to the top and down the steep descent on the other side (with the view ahead of you all the way) to the first junction left which you take. As you can see from the map this road runs south-east and then north-east back to Castle Donovan. It is a pleasant but not very exciting 2.5 mile stretch which passes through fertile farming countryside. Keep straight ahead wherever there is a junction to the right. About 0.5 mile from the end there is a pleasant view of the castle, Nowen and Milane Hill.

Distance: 4.25 miles. Time: 2.5 hours.

A suggested long circular walk incorporating the Bantry old road, Lough Bofinna and the Gowlane road

Starting again from Castle Donovan take off on the Bantry old road and when you get to the left turn referred to in the previous suggested walk keep straight ahead. Here the road has lost most of its height and, hence, its views though glimpses of the surroundings of Bantry Bay are snatched here and there. After a somewhat dull 2.5 miles you arrive at the north-east corner of Lough Bofinna (always blue and peaceful and a delightful spot for a rest). Here you turn right on the narrow road up the hill towards the north. As the road continues to rise you get good views of Bantry Bay, now much closer and, more or less on the same level as yourself. Having passed the highest point you are confronted with an entirely new and very fine view to the north towards the Maughanaclea Hills and further off, the heights of Coomhola. Just as you pass through a grove of trees there is a very fine standing stone up on your left ahead.

After a further short gradual descent you turn right at a T junction (about 6 miles from the start). You are now in the Mealagh Valley with the wide valley floor on your left and the heights of Mullaghmesha on you right and with over 3

119

miles of not very exciting scenery ahead of you on a level road. At Gowlane it is impossible to miss your turn to the right onto the steeply rising Gowlane road.

Distance 12.5 miles. Time 4 hours.

This is a good long walk but almost half of it is not very exciting, though pleasant. On the other hand, however, the good stretches are great. On balance it is worth it for a good day's outing.

25

The Priestsleap

This walk is truly a situation where the best wine is kept till the last. It is only about 8.5 miles. It starts virtually at sea level and in 4 miles rises to 1531 ft and then slowly falls to about 300 ft From beginning to end it is grand in the true sense of the word.

As presented here it is not a circle walk and to walk there and back in a day would be a bit much for the average walker. However, at the conclusion of the account some suggestions will be offered in regard to 'transport'.

The course of the walk is best indicated by pointing out the starting and finishing points on the map (Sheet 24). The former is about 0.75 mile north-west of Snave Bridge (G.R: V 999 544) which is on the N71 that runs from Cork to Skibbereen in the south-west and thence to Bantry, Glengarriff, Kenmare and Killarney. The latter is at Bunane church (G.R. V 940 638) in Co. Kerry and is again on the N71. You can now trace the route where it is shown as a blend of third-class and 'other' road running roughly north and crossing the Cork–Kerry border at Priestsleap and then descending into Kerry, swinging west and ultimately joining the N71 near Bunane Bridge. The Youth Hostel which is marked on the map is now closed. The church is indicated by the conventional +.

The entire route is clearly marked on the Sheet 24. However it is also on the 1in. District Map of Killarney.[1] It is worth bringing along the latter as the detail is that much better. Furthermore if you have the Ireland–South sheet bring that along too because it covers the great view to the north and west from Priestsleap.

One is about to walk here on the old road between Bantry and Kenmare and, on the 1in map you can trace it the whole way to Kenmare as it follows down the eastern bank of the Sheen river whereas today's main road (N71) takes the

---

[1] *Published by the Ordnance Survey of Ireland.*

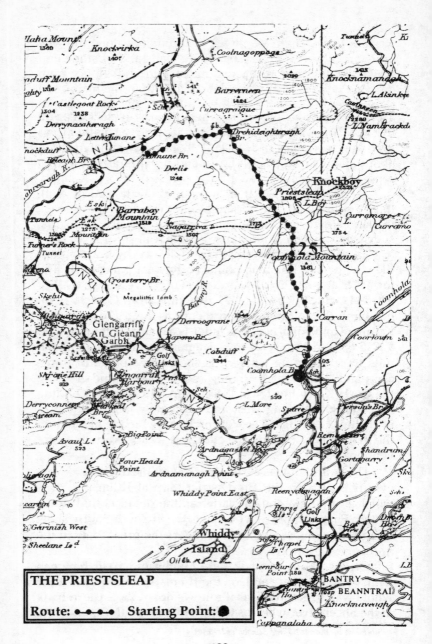

THE PRIESTSLEAP

Route: ●━●━●━●   Starting Point: ●

western bank. There are plenty of reminders along the way of its age – traces of very old stone walls and of stone embankments to support it across marshy ground. Notice from the map how ever so much shorter it is than the main road reminding one again that the walker of the past did not mind the steep gradient as long as it shortened the distance.

As to the origin of the name 'Priestsleap' the story is told that in penal times a priest on horseback away up near Knockboy was being pursued by crown forces who would capture him and put him to death. Just as they were catching up on him the horse took off and flew with its rider through the air away down to near Bantry town.

Two points worth noting at this stage. Time was when the upper reaches of the walk on both the Cork and Kerry sides were rough going. Recently Cork County Council has made considerable improvements on its side – widening here and there, passing points and parking bays for cars but so far no new tarmacadaming. The intention is obviously to develop its tourist potential for car drivers and lessen its pleasure for walkers. Hence, the sooner you walk it the better. Secondly pick your day carefully to ensure that you get the best out of those great distant views – sunny with well dispersed cloud and a light northerly breeze and above all no haze or mist. Ideally it should be walked after a spell of rain when the many cascading rivers and streams are in spate.

If you are coming to Snave from Macroom the most convenient route to take is the R584 via Inchigeelagh and Kealkil to Ballylickey Cross at the head of Bantry Bay where you join the N71 for the 1.5 mile stretch north to Snave. If you are travelling from Cork the shortest and fastest route is via the Macroom road, N22 to 0.5 mile west of Farnanes where you turn left onto the R585 signposted to Bantry/Glengarriff. This will take you via Cappeen and Cousane Gap to Kealkil where you join the R584. Incidentally this is a very fine route for scenery especially from Cappeen on where you have good broad views of the Shehy range and where, at Cousane Gap, you pass over a shoulder of Shehy mountain itself. Having crossed Snave bridge you turn right at the signpost to Kilgarvan. After about 0.75 mile on a pleasant wooded road with the Coomhola river on your right you arrive at Coomhola Bridge (named on Sheet 24 but not on the 1 in. map) where, near the post-office/shop you will see the sign-posted Priestsleap road (you do not cross Coomhola Bridge) and this is where the walk begins. Park the car opposite the shop.

A right turn at the second signpost to Priestsleap brings you onto a gradually rising road through fairly dense foliage. On the left notice the eastern looking figures in bas-relief on the gate pillars of Coomhola Lodge. As the road continues to rise the foliage becomes thinner and the home-steads fewer. After a mile or so it is thin enough to allow good views to the right of Doughill, Douce and Shehy and – slightly to the fore – the high land around Bull's Pocket (walk 23). As you come into open country and pass the last cluster of homesteads the gradient steepens.

To the left can be seen the rounded top of Cobduff (1,244 ft) and the unnamed peak of 1,544 ft with green fertile fields on their lower slopes which give way to the broadened valley of the Cooleenlemane river. Very soon the view to the right is cut off as the road climbs higher and into the lee of Coomhola mountain. However the view to the left continues to become more and more spectacular since you have now risen well up on the eastern shoulder of the Cooleenlemane valley and away below you the river meanders now between boulder and now between green pasture. Although the floor of the valley is long since bereft of homesteads, the good alluvial soil is still worked.

And now, perhaps it is time to look back at that fine view across the upper reaches of Bantry Bay with Bantry it-self nestling in the north-eastern corner. Up behind it are the heights of Mullaghmesha (Walk 24). As your eye moves to the right the peninsula of Muntervary stretches before you. This is the high peninsula (with Sheep's Head at its ocean end) which separates Bantry Bay and Dunmanus Bay to the south. Looking over the peninsula one can clearly see Mount Gabriel and away to the west Carn Ui Neid, the high point above Mizen Head. To the left of Mount Gabriel over the lower land one can see the waters of Roaringwater Bay and beyond on the skyline the outline of Clear Island. This is a great view which you have with you right to the top and the higher you climb the better it becomes. Notice the clusters of old trees here and there below. Time was, perhaps, when the entire valley was covered in trees.

You can now see the road zig-zagging away ahead of you as it makes for the top at a slight dip through which it passes into Kerry. The Cooleenlemane Valley is now becoming quite shallow and it is rising up to road level. About 0.5 mile from the top you come close to its actual head just on your left and this is another good spot to look back down along the entire length of the valley onto where it widens before the river joins the Coomhola river not far from the walk's starting point. It is perhaps hard to believe that in fairly recent geological time a glacier moved down this valley, conferring on it a U-shaped cross section in place of a V.

Passing the little iron cross on your left you reach the top (1.5–2 hours from the start) and suddenly that breathtaking vista of the distant Kerry mountains bursts upon you. Straight ahead (towards the north-west) is the best view you will ever get of the entire MacGillycuddy's Reeks crowned by the three highest peaks – Carrauntoohil (3,414 ft), Beenkeragh (3,314 ft), and Caher (3,200 ft). To the right and separated from them by the Gap of Dunloe are Purple Mountain and Tomies Mountain while further still to the right the flat top of Mangerton stands out. Away to your left (west) are all the peaks of the Iveragh peninsula with crooked Coomacarrea (2,541 ft) presiding over all. The immediate foreground is much more barren and desolate than that of the other side and one can see the road ahead falling away to the distant green fields. It is well worth scrambling up from the road to the top of the crag on the left-hand side for the sake of enjoying both great views together and contrasting one with the other. This is surely another one of those places where it is good to be.

And now for the splendid walk down the track to the Sheen river which flows north into Kenmare Bay. The great view of the Kerry mountains stays right ahead of you for at least 2 miles and while you are still up high a look to the left here and there will reveal the peaks of the Caha and Slieve Miskish ranges which make up the Beara peninsula. Up on the right behind you is Knockboy (2,321 ft) from the slopes of which you can see the Coomeelan stream descending and ultimately closing with the road and crossing it at Drehidoughteragh (Droichead Uachtarach – Upper Bridge) close to the first homestead you have seen for about 5 miles. There can be superb cascades in the stream on either side of this old stone bridge. Incidentally the high wooded plateau over on your left is Deelis (1,242 ft).

You are now down into fairly fertile country with trees bordering the road but yet there are glimpses of those magnificent Kerry mountains. About 0.5 mile down from the bridge you come to another bridge Drehideighteragh (Droichead Iochtarach – Lower Bridge) where another cascading stream crosses your track. Very shortly the road (surfaced for about 0.5 mile back) swings left and is joined by a surfaced road coming in on the right. This point is indicated on the map by a triangle of roads which has now disappeared. Soon you pass on your right a signpost to 'Burial Ground'. This is indicated on the map by 'Church' in Gothic script and a cross. For about 0.5 mile from here on the road winds and undulates through pleasant foliage until you come to a T junction.

Care must be exercised here not to go wrong by confusing this junction with the one about 200 yards ahead. This first junction is between the road on which you are and a surfaced road on the left which is indicated on the map by a mere dotted line and which wanders up a valley and ends at a homestead. Therefore at this first junction turn right and at the next junction you turn left on a minor road which almost immediately crosses the Coomeelan stream shortly above its confluence with the Sheen river.

The road on which you now are comprises a mile of delightful walking as it runs south-west along the shoulder of the Sheen valley with the heights of Deelis on the left. There are no occupied homesteads along here, hence the green spine extends right across the width of the road in places. As you walk along in the shade of old trees you get some fine views of the Caha mountains ahead and to the right and in the foreground, of the Sheen river. Soon you will see Bunane Church ahead on the right and shortly after you have come in line with it you pick up your junction right which takes you over the Sheen (picture-postcard view from the left-hand parapet of the bridge) and up through green rocky pasture to the main road with the church opposite you.

Distance: (from Coomhola) 8.5–9 miles. Time: approximately 3.5–4 hours.

A point worth noting here is the following: from the map there would appear to be a promising walk by turning left just before you turn right to cross Bunane bridge and taking the road up by Barraboy Mountain and along by the forestry on Esk Mountain down to the Cork side of the N71 main road. Certainly the road up from the bridge is well worthwhile. As it rises it goes into wilder and wilder country and eventually peters out and one has to cross rough damp terrain to pick up the muddy track near the forestry. Not recommended except for the experienced cross-country walker.

And now for a few suggestions regarding vehicular transport. You could of course drive your car across the whole walk from Coomhola to Bunane but you would lose all the magic of this great walk in addition to being an irritation to any genuine walkers and your car may not like the treatment it would get. The ideal arrangement is to be dropped off at Coomhola and collected at Bunane church some 4–5 hours later. In other words, car plus driver come from one point to the other via N71 (15 miles) while you walk it via Priestsleap (i.e. 8.5 miles). An alternative would be to make 2 walks out of it on two separate occasions; one up the Cork side and back leaving the car at Coomhola and the other up the Kerry side and back leaving your car at Bunane on the main road in front of the church where there is ample parking.

Conclusion

Conclusion to this booklet, yes but hopefully not to your walking in West Cork and beyond. If you have 'done' all of the 25 walks once you will have walked about 200 miles (320 km). This is but a small fraction of the total mileage of by-road in the area and having done these walks you should be sufficiently familiar with the area and with its represent-ation on map to plan some walks of your own. Why not fol-low up some of those little roads which you passed at junc-tions and which looked so attractive? Why not venture up some more of those 'turf roads'. Mostly they are cul-de-sacs but they will go up high and afford superb views. Why not explore some of that magnificent coastline seen on some of the later walks.

Go then to the 'West Country. It is composite country; no majestic peaks or ultra-pastoral river valleys but a com-bination of both extremes intermingled in an almost Japan-ese miniature landscape garden manner. There is no over-stressing of one land form to make even an hour's trip monotonous'.[1]

---

[1] J.C. Coleman, *Journeys into Muskerry*.